JN417885

Copyrighted Material
Melodies of Quiescence:
Selected Poems & Prose of Won-gil Kim

Published by
Yeungnam University Press
2022

214-1, Gyeongsan City,
Gyeongsangbuk-do, Republic of Korea
(Tel) 053-810-1801-4 (Fax) 053-810-4722
http://book.yu.ac.kr

First published
5 July 2022

Poems in Korean Texts
© Won-gil Kim
English translations
© Jeo-yong Noh

US$ 21.00
₩27.000

Book Design: Jae-wan Jeong
jjwankk@gmail.com

ISBN 978-89-7581-855-4 03810

All right Reserved.
No part of this publication may be reproduced,
stored in retrieval system, or transmitted in any form, or
by any means, electronic, mechanical, photocopying, recording
or otherwise, without the written permission of the publisher
except for brief passages quoted in a review.

Copyrighted Material

Selected Poems & Prose of
Won-gil Kim

Melodies of Quiescence

Parallel Texts in
Korean and English
Translated by
Jeo-yong Noh

The Poet's Preface

A Korean language dictionary defines "jeokmak" (寂寞) as tranquillity or desolation. Tranquillity is close to serenity in meaning, but the word "jeokmak" is near to desolation with a nuance of loneliness. It also connotes quiescence, a temporary cessation of activity or existence. A man may tend to evade a state of quiescence, while preferring tranquillity to a temporary cessation of existence. However, if one comes to relish a supreme moment of quiescence, cessation in action, and gets acquainted with it, he attains a sense of detachment from the mundane affairs and eventually gets to a far-sighted view of life. Quiescence implies a sudden awakening after a momentary arrest as in a Buddhist meditation of "seon" (禪). It is a sort of enlightenment. In my view, quiescence was in the beginning of the world. Perhaps, it may demand one's lifetime to acknowledge the adage: "Life begins from quiescence and ends with quiescence."

For this volume, I have chosen a total of seventy-three poems related directly or indirectly to the various themes of quiescence from my complete works. Some poems are thematically related to a sadness of loneliness or longingness or parting or remorse. Others are related to a painful cry of wandering or despair or a placidity of resignation or meditation or quiescence as in an elevated state of philosophical speculation. On the way from a superficial level of quiescence to a deep level, I have displayed a diverse range of emotional experiences through looking back over the bygone days.

The word "haeng" (行) from the title "Jeokmakhaeng" (寂寞行) denotes travelling as in case of going to Seoul or Busan, It is also used to refer to a lyrical song in Chinese poems such as in "The Song of a Juvenile" (少年行) by Li Po or "The Pipa Song" (琵琶行) by Bo Juyi. Thus, the word "haeng" combines a sense of journey with a lyrical song.

I wish to express my sincere gratitude to Dr. Jeo-yong Noh for his tireless efforts for accurate rendering my poems into English. I believe that his excellent translations of my works have made them easily accesible to English readers. Also, my grateful acknowledgements are due to Mr. Jongbaek Lee, Editor-in-Chief of the Yeungnam University Media and Press Center, who has been patient until the manuscript corrections were satisfactorily made.

June in 2022

Won-gil Kim

Acknowledgements

The translator wishes to express his deep gratitude to the poet Won-gil Kim who has helped the translator to understand his poems through close contacts in dialogues and by exchanging numerous e-mails to ensure that the translated poems are both accurate and poetic as in the original poems. As the translator wrote in his previous volume of translated poems, *Birds, Flowers, and Men*, this volume has been also produced with the same assumption that it is the translator's aim in translating poetry to be faithfully accurate to the original text and at the same time to make translations read well as poems in their own right. This dual aim has not been always easy to maintain and sometimes has turned out to be contradictory. In that case, the translator has tried to evade the word-for-word translation with a belief that a translated work is not a shadow of an original text but a newly created work.

The translator also wishes to express his grateful acknowledgement to Professor Park Taekyung, Director of the Yeungnam University Media and Press Center, who has encouraged the translator by giving an opportunity to render Korean literary texts into English and Professor Jae-wan Jeong from the Dept of Visual Communication Design for his design of this book. Finally, acknowledgements are due to the staff of the Yeungnam Unversity Media and Press Center, who have made every effort to bring out this book to the world.

A Note on the Original Text

This volume of translation is based on the original text titled *Jeokmakhaeng* (寂寞行), the revised second edition of the same title. The first edition was published by Cheongeo in Seoul in 2020. A year later, the revised second edition was published by Siseonsa in Seoul. By examining the two texts, the second edition turns out to be considerably different from the first edition. For example, the first edition contains eighty-one poems, but the second edition is reduced to sixty-six. Structurally, the first edition is divided into five parts, but the second edition has four parts and concentrates on a variety of themes of quiescence. Apart from these structural differences, there are many substantial changes from the first edition in the second edition. The poet himself believes that the second edition is the finest one at present. As he divulged himself elsewhere, he has such an odd habit of a constant revision of the text after publication. He appears to be never completely satisfied with his own finished work. For this volume of translation, the poet insists strongly that the second edition of *Jeokmakhaeng* on which this translation is based is an ideal copy, meaning the most complete and perfect copy possible of an issue of his printed books.

Table of Contents

2부 Part Two

3부 Part Three

4부 Part Four

1부
Part One

벚꽃 아래서

꽃이 흔들린다.
바람이 부나부다.

슬픔일까.
벽에 비쳐 일렁이는 물무늬같이
여리게 가슴에 와 일렁이는 것은.

꽃방울에 드나드는
벌같이
감상(感傷)이
내 짙은 이마에, 감은 눈두덩에
와서 지분거린다.

따스한 봄날
그런대로 화사한 꽃그늘에서
까닭 없이 잠기는
이 우수(憂愁)의 버릇은

울다 잠든
아기의 추스림같이
철 지난 서름의 가녀린 여운(餘韻)일까,

Under the Cherry Blossoms

Blossoms are stirring.
The wind seems to be blowing.

Is it sadness,
like a pattern of rippling water reflected on the wall,
which undulates tenderly on my heart?

Like a bee
flitting from a flowerbud to a flowerbud,
a sentiment on my forehead felt
and fallen on my closed eyelids
makes me annoyed.

On a balmy spring day
in the shade of the florid flowers,
a habit of being lost in melancholy
for naught is,

like a baby's pulling itself together
by falling asleep after crying,
a fine lingering sadness out of season?

저만치 흔들리는
꽃을 볼 뿐인데.

It's just to watch blossoms
stirring at that far distance.

환영(幻影)

저무는 강나루
적막을 보듯
여인은 스잔한 눈빛을 하고

나직이 울리는
물 젖은 음성,
연잎에 도닥이며 비 내리는 소리.

환영은
빛 맑은 초상(肖像)만은 아니네.
갈숲에서 울다 온 바람결 내음. . .

추회(追懷)는
허옇게 무리진 안개 되어 내리고.

비 먹은 나무처럼
흠뻑
젖어 있는 나

An Apparition

At a darkling ferry,
as if caught sight of dreariness,
a woman has forlorn eyes.

Resonating low
in a damp voice:
a dripping of rainfall on lotus leaves.

An apparition
is not only a clear reflection but the smell
of a wind coming crying among the reeds . . .

Retrospection
falls down in the whitish dense mist.

Like a soaked tree
dripping,
I was wet.

마법

그리운 율리아나,
어이 할거나,
나는 몹쓸 저주에 걸려
여자의 사랑만이 사슬을 푼다는
별난 마법에 걸려
괴물의 몸으로 빈 성에 숨어 사는
이야기 속 딱한 왕자.

율리아나, 그대 또한
멀리 외져 발길 없는 숲 속 궁전,
백년을 옴짝 않고 누워 잠자니
내 입김 고운 뺨에 닿기만 해도
저승같이 깊은 잠 깨어날 텐데
어이 할거나, 나도 그대도
어이 할거나, 이 마법.

Magic

My dear Juliana,
what shall I do?
I fell under a weired spell;
a lady's love can only break the spell.
I am a pitiful prince in a tale,
dwelling as a monster hidden
in an empty castle.

Juliana,
in a far remote palace in the woods,
you have also slept for a hundred years.
If my breath once touches your sweet cheek,
you will wake up from an otherworldly deep sleep.
What shall I do? You and I,
what shall we do with this spell?

고향

산에 들에 나니는 새들
유변나게 마음 가는 꽃가지 있듯
세상을 팔난봉으로 헤매다녀도
돌아가 쉬고 싶은 고향 있었네

Hometown

As there is a favorite flowering twig to perch on
for a bird flittering over mountains and fields,
one may roam around the world as a rake,
yet there is a hometown he wishes to return for a rest.

경포(鏡浦)[°]를 지나며

친구여 자네도
시월 저녁 일곱 시 쯤
경포 앞 남행길을 버스로 지나면서
노을이 물든 가을 강을
본 적 있는가.

자네도 이 사람,
어스름 물굽이에 눈을 주다가
아득하니 잊어버린
옛사랑의 이름,
느닷없이 나직하게 불러 본 적 있는가.

새삼스레 멋쩍어 낯을 붉히고
불러본 적 있는가, 씁쓰라니 옛이름,
불혹 넘은 나이에
불러 본 적 있는가.

° 경포: 지명. 안동 내앞마을 서쪽, 반변천의 풍광이 빼어난 소호(沼湖).

Passing by Gyeongpo°

My dear chum,
have you seen too
around 7 pm in October,
the autumn river tinted with an evening glow,
while going southward by bus before Gyeongpo?

My dear friend,
glancing at the curve of the dusky river,
have you ever called unawares your old love
by name in a low voice
that you had forgot long ago?

Blushing afresh,
have you ever called the old name wryly
at over forty years old
and have you ever called it?

° Gyeongpo is the name of a place located in the west of Naeap village, Andong city. The small marsh in the Banbyeon river is noted for its natural scenic beauty.

분홍 신

—옛날 영화

모이라 사라
중학생 때 문화교실 '분홍 신'에 나온
주연 여자 배우 모이라 시어러.
그 아득한 이름이 문득
입술에 맴돌다니!

사람이 발끝으로 서서 춤추는 걸
그때 서양 영화 속에서 처음 보았지.
사랑과 예술 사이에서 어쩌지 못하고
분홍신 신고 무대에서 하염없이 춤추다가
기진하여 죽는 것도 처음 보았지.

얼굴은 잊었지만 생생한 장면,
달빛 교교히 일렁이는 호수
호숫가 숲 속 길로 은장식 쌍두마차
마차 속 연인들은 호수를 내다보고
마차 위의 마부는 졸고 있고. . .

그날 이후, 나는 정말이지
그런 숲길, 그런 호수를 갖고 싶었다.
달 아래 은물결 보고 싶었다.

The Red Shoes°

—An old movie

Moira Sara
who came on for the middle school 'culture class'°°
was the heroine, Moira Shearer, in *The Red Shoes*.
Surprisingly, the old name pops up
unawares in my mind!

It was the first time that I saw a woman
dancing on her tiptoe in a western movie.
Firstly, I also saw the woman dying of exhaustion,
not knowing what to do between love and art,
while dancing unceasingly on the stage in her red shoes.

Though her face is forgotten, scenes remain vivid
in my memory; the lake rippling in moonlight,
a two-horse carriage adorned in silver
    that runs along a woodland path by the lake,
lovers in the carriage were looking across the lake,
while the groom on the carriage was dozing...

Since that day, I have really wished to own
such a woodland path and a lake.

사십 년 전 '분홍 신'의 그 장면처럼
달빛 어린 호숫가 거닐고 싶다.

I also wished to watch silvery ripples
    on the moonlit lake.
As in the movie that I watched forty years ago,
I wish to stroll along the lake in moonlight.

°The movie, "The Red Shoes", is a 1948 British drama film which marked the feature film debut of Moira Shearer. It is a story about a girl who is torn between the man she loves and her pursuit of a prima ballerina. The heroine, Moira Shearer, was an internationally well-known Scottish ballet dancer and actress. She died at the age of 80 in Oxford in 2006.

°°Under the name of the "culture class", students in middle school were supervised to watch a certified film in a public cinema house as part of cultural education in the 50s.

애염명왕(愛染明王)

저 인도 불교의 하나인
진언밀교(眞言密敎)에는
애염명왕이라 하는 멋쟁이 신(神)이 있다지
눈이 셋
팔이 여섯
머리엔 사자관(獅子冠)에
온몸이 붉다 하니
우리네 옛 얘기 속 도깨비보다도
더 무섭고 더 밉것다.
헌데 밖으론 이처럼 분노의 정을 나타내나
내심 어쩔 수 없는 사랑을 가진 신(神)
애욕을 본체(本體)로 하는 사랑의 신이라나.

프랑스 동화 '미녀와 야수'에도 있지.
빈 궁전에 홀로 사는 괴물이 있어서
보는 이마다 까무러칠 정도였지만
가슴속엔 한없이 슬픈 사랑을 지녀
맘씨 고운 처녀의 사랑을 얻자
아름답고 씩씩한 왕자로 변했다지.

Rágarája°

In Indian esoteric and Vajrayana Buddhist
traditions, it is said there is a dandyish deity
known as a *Love-stained Wisdom King*.
He has three eyes,
six arms,
and a lion-carved crown
with his red body.
So he must be more terrifying
or homelier than a goblin in our old tales.
Outwardly, he exposes such a feeling of wrath;
yet inwardly, he is a deity incubating inevitable lust
and professing love as an entity of his existence.

The French tale *Beauty and the Beast* has it:
in an empty palace, a monster lived alone.
Whoever saw him, the viewer was almost fainted,
though.
With a boundless sad love in his heart,
after he won love from an innocent maid

° Rāgarāja was originally a Hindu diety and known to transform worldly lust into spiritual awakening. In China, the Sanskrit name was literally translated as *Àirǎn Míngwángna* "Love-stained Wisdom King".

여인의 참된 사랑 받기만 하면
흉한 허물 훌렁 벗게 되는
별나고도 끔찍한 마법에 걸려 있던
팔자 애꿎은 왕자였다지.

우리 모두 잘 아는 노트르담의 종지기
곱추야 대순가 귀머거리에다가
귀먹은 거야 대순가 벙어리에다가
끝내주게 못생긴 콰지모도란 녀석,
오직 순정만이
오직 의리와 순정만이
춤추는 집시 여자 에스메랄다를
영혼 깊숙이 울려놓은 거 있지
그녀 죽자 동굴에 안고 가 그 곁에 눈 감고
뼈 다 삭을 때까지 함께 손잡고
삭은 뼈가 바람에 뒤엉키도록. . .

and turned into an apothic, brave prince.
Once he was truly loved by the maid,
he stripped off a hedious foreskin
and transformed himself into a prince
who was fallen under a weird, ill-fated spell.

We all know there is a bell-ringer of Notre Dame.
What's so special about the hunchback? He is also deaf.
What is so special about deafness? He is also a mute
and a grotesque Qasimodo.
Only a genuine love,
only fidelity or a pure love
can appeal to the deepest soul
of the dancing gipsy, Esmeralda[°°].
After her death, he took her to a cave,
lied down beside her and closed his eyes
until his gripping hands turned to the dust
and the dust got mixed by the wind.

[°°] She is a young woman belonging to an oppressed group known as gypsies. Esmeralda is an outspoken humanitarian, which drives her to protect the deformed bell-ringer, Quasimodo, from his oppressors namely, Minister Frollo.

우리 고구려의 바보 온달(溫達)
일자무식 산중 촌놈, 천지에 소문난 바보.
오죽하면 그 바보 대궐까지 알게 되어
울보공주 나무랄 적 '온달에게 보내겠다.'
아, 그것이 그 큰 그리움의 싹 될 줄이야
공주 덕에 글 깨치고 사랑 덕에 무술 배워
오랑캐 쳐부수러 갑옷 입고 말을 타고
긴 창 잡고 출정(出征)할 때
배웅하는 공주 가슴 얼마나 벅찼을까!
장수되어 나라 지킨 온달 장군.

우리 신라의 선덕여왕(善德女王)
불공(佛供) 드리는 데까지 따라다니던
사랑에 미친 사내, 지귀(志鬼).
봉두난발(蓬頭亂髮)에 남루를 걸치고
절 마당 탑 그늘에 지쳐 잠든 지귀.
여왕이 가슴에 얹어 준 금팔찌 알아보고
아, 그 기쁨에 몸에서 불이 나서
아암, 나고 말고, 꽃불이 나서

The blockheaded Ondal from Goguryeo[○○○];
he was a hillbilly, a reputed idiot in the world.
So, he was notoriously known to the royal court.
When a princess was chided for her crying, she was told
she would be sent to Ondal for marriage.
Ah, who could guess that was the seed of
her earnest longing for him.
By dint of the princess, Ondal became literate,
by dint of love, he learnt a martial art.
When he went to war against the barbarians
in armour and on horseback with a long lance,
how full was her heart with pride when she saw him off!
He turned into the general who protected the country,

Queen Seondeok[○○○○] from Silla.
There was Jigui who was madly in love with her.
He trod on the heels of her who went to a temple
to pray.

[○○○] One of the kingdoms founded in the northern part of the Korean peninsula and China in 37 BC and destroyed by the kingdom of Silla in 668.

[○○○○] Queen Seondeok who reigned between 632 and 647 in Silla Kingdom is the first queen in the history of Korea. She was the 27th queen of Silla Kingdom.

뛰고 춤추고 춤추며 뛰어선
육신을 다 사루어 열반입멸(涅槃入滅)하였지.

오늘은 어쩌자고 지지리 못난 자들만
하나 둘 문득문득 떠오르는가
그 모양 그 꼴로도 사랑 가진 것들만
그 모양 그 꼴로도 사랑 받은 것들만
떠오르는가.

그대 가고 없는 지금
떠오르는가!

Waiting for the queen in unkempt hair and raggs
to have a grimpse at her,
he fell into sleep in the shadow of a tower in the court-
yard.
Wakened up, he sensed the queen's bracelet on his bo-
som.
Ah, in a blissful rapture, his body was set on fire.
Oh, yes, it was on fire. Truly, it was burning on fire,
so he leaped while dancing—danced while leaping.
He burnt up himself and then passed into nirvana.

Today, why on earth does such a foolhead run
across my mind one after another!
Only, those who had a pure love in such a look
and those who were loved by such a look
run across my mind!

Why they run across my mind,
after you are not here and gone now!

하늘

구름자락 걷히고
바람 자는 날
풀 언덕에 홀로 누워 하늘을 보면
아스라이 새파란 하늘을 보면
알 만하구나.

저 가 없는 허망을
머리에 이고 있는 한
인생은 자나 깨나 우주의 바닷가에
혼자 있구나.

원시적 떠돌던 인간의 조상들이
맨 처음 바다를 만나
뜻 모를 수평 앞에 느낀 것도
이런 걸까?

가을 하늘 어지러이 깊어 뵈는 날
풀 언덕에 홀로 누워 하늘을 보면
알 만하구나.

이브는 다 달랠 수 없는
아담의
외롬.

The Sky

On a day when a fringe of clouds is gone
and the wind dies down,
lying back alone on the grassy fell
and looking up at the sky—the azure blue sky,
I think I know.

As far as I carry
an endless vanity on my head,
life stays alone day and night
on the shore of the universe.

When our primeval nomadic ancestors
encountered the sea for the first time,
what they felt in face of an illegible horizon
was just like this?

On a day when the autumn sky
looks dizzingly deep, I gaze into it
while lying alone. I think I know.

Eve who cannot be cajoled at all
is nothing but
Adam's loneliness.

별후(別後)

물은
거기서
이리 흐르고
달
여기 떠서
그리로 진다.

바람이 오가고
구름 영 넘어
가고
오누나만

오고 갈 줄
모르는
사람.

그대는 거기서
꽃 피는 것 보고
나
여기서
잎 지는 것 본다.

After Parting

Water
flows
thither to hither.
The moon
rises up here
and wanes there.

The wind comes and goes:
a cloud passes over
a mountain ridge
and turns up, though.

You are one
who knows not
about coming and going.

There
you see
flowers blooming:
here
I am

세월은 흐르고
머리카락
한 올
두 올
희어 가는데

가고 올 줄
모르는
사람.

watching leaves falling.
Time flies;
one
or two
strands of hair
turn to grey, though.

You are one
who knows not
about going and coming.

바다로 가며

멀리
산과 산 사이로
호수처럼 뵈는
바다,

여신(女神)의 젖가슴 사이
잔잔히 일렁이는
청옥(靑玉)

바다여
어서 날
한 마리 돌고래나
되게 해 다오.

Going to the Sea

In the far distance
between the mountains,
the sea is looming
like a lake.

Between the bosom of a goddess,
a blue jade
is rippling.

Sea,
let me turn into
a dolphin
at once.

친구 무덤가에서

살아 누운 것과 죽어 누운 게 무어 다른가.
친구 녀석 무덤가에 나란히 누워
강아지풀 입에 문 채 눈 감아 본다.
나 일어날 때, 벗이여, 그대도 깨어나게나.

At the Graveside of My Crony

What's the difference between lying down alive
    and lying down dead?
By the grave of my crony, I lie down abreast,
clinching a foxtail in my teeth and closing my eyes.
When I get up, my dear fellow, you wake up as well.

버들꽃

벗이여,
간밤엔 창 밖의 버들가지 사이로
아, 때 아닌 눈이 오나 했더니

이 아침 햇살 아래
뜰 가득 솜꽃이 하얗게 쌓여
이른 겨울 첫 눈 보듯
눈이 부시네.

허나 보게,
이는 크게 이별 지어 떠나갈 것들,
한 마당 졸업식장 아이들처럼
바람결에 뿔뿔이 흩어질 것들. . .

거스르지 못할 물결에 흘러간
벗이여, 그대는
어디메 뿌릴 내렸나,

나는 잠시
여기 머무네.

Willow Catkins

My old friend,
last night, among willow twigs outside the window,
I deemed, ah, the untimely snow was falling down.

Below this morning's sunbeam,
the garden is filled with downy white flowers.
As if watching the first snowfall in early winter,
I was dazzled.

Yet, look,
these are things to leave in large groups,
like school children at a graduation ceremony,
and scattering in the wind. . .

Dear old friend,
who was swept away by an irresistable current,
where did you take root?

For a while,
here I stay.

징

내 가슴 속 해맑은 순금빛 징 하나
꽃잎에 부딪혀도 무늬 고운 소리 나더니
친구의 누님에겐 왜 빌려줬나
함부로 두들겨서 다 깨어 놨네

A Gong

In my heart, I had a golden glint gong.
When it bumped into the petals, it used
    to let out a lovely patterned sound.
Why on earth did I lend it to my friend's sister?
She broke it into pieces by banging recklessly.

남풍 불면

남풍 속엔 어이 해
겨자 냄새 나는가
코에 스며 눈물 나는
여자 냄새 나는가

나 돌아 못 가네
나 돌아 못가

나무젓가락 나뉘 듯
둘로 나뉜 몸
나는 이리 흘러 와
뿌릴 내렸네.

남풍이 불면야
그냥 못 있어
혼자서 들이키는
쓰거운 술잔.

When the South Wind Blows

How come the south wind smells
of mustard? –
coming into a nose and bringing tears
    to eyes,
why does it smell of a woman?

I won't detour
and won't.

As if a wooden chopstick were split,
we were divided into two.
I migrated hither
and took root.

When the south wind blows,
I can't just stay put.
So, I drink alone
a glass of bitter wine.

폭풍의 언덕

—옛날 영화

주워 온 아이 히스클리프 역을
로렌스 올리비에가 하고 있었다.

철없는 소녀의 상심의 말 한마디
소년은 집을 떠난다.
'그래, 내가 떠남으로써
네가 날 사랑한다는 것 깨닫게 해 줄 거야'.

그래, 나도 그녀를 떠나왔고
그로부터 모든 게
어긋나고 말았지

그녀도 가엾은 캐서린처럼
애증의 세월을 울고 웃다가

지금쯤 죽었을까,
살아 있을까?

무섭게 폭풍 부는 어둔 밤이면
창밖에 누군가 울부짖는 것만 같다.

Wuthering Heights

—An old movie

Lawrence Olivier was starring
as Heathcliff, a foundling.

The boy hurt by a word of the rash maid
leaves Wuthering Heights.
All right. By departing, I'll make you realize
you are in love with me, he declared.

Yes, I also left her.
Thereafter,
everything has gone awry.

I wonder whether she has cried or laughed
for years of hatred like poor Catherine.

By now, is she dead
or alive?

Whenever a fierce storm blows in the dark night,
someone seems likely to howl outside the window.

라 트라비아타

베르디의 어느 음악을 들으면
나로 인(因)하여 박명(薄命)하여가는
여자의 눈물이 보인다.

후미진 뒷거리
성에 낀 창가에 몸을 누이고,
낮빛같이 흰 수건에
동백을 토하는,

아니면
파랗게 깎은 머리를 달빛에 쪼이며
풍경 우는 절 마당을
매돌고 있는지. . .

어쩌면 나처럼
흙바람 눈을 찌르는
생활의 가두(街頭)에서
구겨진 지전(紙錢)을
간추리고 섰는가!

La Traviata

Listening to a snatch of music by Verdi,
I can see a woman shedding tears
and leading an ill-fated life because of me;

at the remote backstreet,
she may lie down by a frosted window
and spit out camellias
on a handkerchief as white as daylight

or
she may bathe her bluish cropped head
    in the moonlight
and linger around the courtyard
of a wind-chiming temple...

or like me
in the street of life
where the dusty wind pokes my eyes,
she may stand
smoothing out creased bills!

그대 이미 어느 산 양지에
백골로 마를지라도, 용서하라
헛된 열을 거느려
참된 하나를 살피지 못한 나를.

기다리는 사람들
다 태우지 못하고 떠나 온
만원(滿員)의 막 버스마냥, 나도
어쩔 수 없었다고나 말하면 될까

베르디를 들으면
내 가슴 울어예는
가을 강 위에
비가 뿌린다.

Though you might have been already dried as a skull
on a sunny side of the mountain, forgive me
not for having cared for a true one,
while taking care of idle ten.

Like the departure of the last jampacked bus
without picking up
all the people waiting for the bus,
can I say it couldn't be helped?

While listening to Verdi,
I feel that rain is strewing
about the autumn river
over which my heart cries.

찔레라도

누구는 가버린 사랑을
이슬에 씻기운 한 송이
장미로 모듬는데

그대 내 가슴에
사철
꽃도 잎도 안 피는
메마른 가시넝쿨로 남아

바람이 일 적마다
서걱
서걱
살을 저민다.

나는 애써
찔레라도 피우고파
찔레라도
피워 가지고파
울어, 눈물로 물 준다만

추억이여,

Even Briar Rose

Someone cuddles a lost love
as a rose
bathed in dew, though;

you stay in my heart
during all four seasons
as a dry thorn vine which
neither blooms nor leaves out.

Whenever the wind rises,
it goes on
rustling
and slicing up my flesh.

With making an effort,
I wish rather to let a briar rose bloom,
nothing but a briar rose,
to have by letting it bloom,
I weep; with tears, I water it, though.

Memory,

한송이 가시 없는 풀꽃으로나
왜
피어 남지 않고.

why you don't keep blooming merely
as a grass flower
without a prickle?

거릿 귀신

자정도 지난 빈 거리를
거닐다 돌아와
빈 방 가운데 서다.

창유리 속에
본 듯한 사내 하나
피곤한 표정
나를 보고 있다.

왜 따라다녀, 하니
왜 따라다녀, 한다.

다시 거리를 나돌다가
버릇처럼 방에 들면
창유리 속의 그 사내가
또 날 보고 있다.

미친 녀석, 했더니
미쳤군, 한 것 같았다.

A Street Goblin

Coming back home after midnight
from a deserted street along which I strolled,
I stand in the middle of a vacant room.

In the window-pane,
a man whom I seem to have seen before
is gazing at me
with a weary look.

Why do you suck around me?,
  I reproached.
He replied, *Why do you suck around me?*

Strolling along the street again,
if I return to the room as I used to,
the man in the window-pane
is watching me again.

A lunatic, I jerked out.
He seems to have retorted, *Lunatic!*.

2부
Part Two

여숙(旅宿)

낮은 천정에는
이제 막
노숙(露宿)에서 돌아온 사나이의
이슬에 젖은 맥고모자가
묵상에 잠긴 듯 걸리어 있고,

'역마(驛馬)'에 쫓기는
핏대 센 사내들이 베고 간
때 묻은 목침이
윗목에 하나.

정 뜬 여자의
등살같이 차가운 흙벽에
무너져 앉아
한숨 섞어 내뿜는 담배
파아란 연기. . .

아직은 책장 덮듯
닫을 수 없는 문 밖으로
눈 들어 흘낏 치어다보면
까닭 없이 서슬 푸른 하늘은
간수(看守)인 양 저만치서 기다리고 섰다.

Lodging

A man has just returned
from an open-air slumber
and his straw hat wet with dew
rests on a low ceiling,
as if lost in meditation.

On the upper side of a room,
there is a grimy wooden-pillow
used by the strong-blooded men
chased by a *post-horse.*

Flopping down
against the cold earthen wall,
like the back muscle of a lovelorn woman,
I puff out
the bluish smoke mingled with a sigh. . . .

When I cast a glance outside the gate
that can't be closed yet like a book,
the menacing sky without reason
stands waiting at some distance away
as if it were a prison warder.

하차(下車)

낯선 도시의 역 광장
가등(街燈) 아래 서면
손가방 든 내가 우습구나.

길은 팔방으로 뻗어
여객은 뿔뿔이 흩어져 가고
나도 주착주착
어디라 갈 곳이나 있다는 듯이. . .

저기 저 길을 건너면
어린 내 웃음과 행복이 피던 골목,
슬픔과 눈물로 떠나온 집.

이 저녁엔 어느 누가
내 손때 묻은 문을 닫고 앉아
한 상 가득 웃음꽃을 피우고 있을까?

팔방으로 뻗어나간 휘황한 길로
사람들은 분주히 돌아가는데
반기는 이 하나 없는
이 텅 빈 거리에
내 무엇 하러 내렸나.

Getting Off

If I stop under a streetlamp
at a station square in an unfamiliar city,
it's silly of me who is carrying a gripsack.

The street stretches in every direction
and travellers are driven asunder;
I myself make a gesture to set out
as if I had my destination.

Across the street over there, there is an alley
where laughter and bliss had burst in my early days;
a house from which I left with sadness and tears.

This evening, who would make laughter
burst out around a dining table,
after shutting out the door soiled by my hand?

People are going back in haste in all directions
stretched to the dazzling streets.
In this vacant street
where not a single soul greets me,
how come I got off?

바다에 던진 모자

VO
VOU
목쉰 뱃고동

쪽빛 물결을
미끄러져 가면
하얀 돛을 단 배가 지나고
귤빛 등을 단 등대 지나고

반도도
대륙도
아물거리다간
석양의 수평 속에 잠기어 가고

사랑도 영웅도
잠기어 가고. . .

VO
VOU
작별을 하자.

A Hat Thrown into the Sea

Vo

Vou,

the throaty sound of a foghorn.

When a ship glides over

the indigo waves,

it passes by a white sailboat

and a lighthouse furnished with a tangerine colour lamp.

A peninsula

or a continent

shimmers

and sinks into the gloaming horizon as well.

Love and heroes

are also sinking . . .

Vo

Vou,

let's bid a farewell.

뭍에서
맘이 상해
바다로 가는 사내,

낡은 모자 하나
빙그르르
하늘 멀리
던져 버린다.

A man whose heart
was broken on the land
is going to sea.

He is throwing
an old hat
twirling around
into the far distant sky.

하와이에 와서

더운 것이 약간 흠이긴 하지만
지상에서 제일 낙원에 가깝다는
뱀 없는 섬 하와이에 와서

가까이 킬라우에 화산의 종작 못할 노염과
대 태풍 대 해일을 기우(杞憂)하여
섬째 물속으로 갈앉는 일 없을까고
자발없이 자발없이 생각해 보는 것은
하와이 살면 어떨까 싶어서다.

태평양 전쟁 때 진주만 피습처럼
소제(蘇製) 핵공격에 당하는 일 없을까고
펀치보울 국립묘지와 다이어먼헤드의
군사기지 볼 때
버섯구름 사진이 떠오르는 것은
여기 새로 뿌리 내리면 어떨까 싶어서다.

바다 건너 고향 마을
산업기지 댐 건설로 수몰되는데
청산도 선영도 다 가라앉고
인걸도 인정도 다 흩어지는데

After Arrival in Hawaii

Though a broiling weather is a small defect
in Hawaii, known as being closest to paradise on earth
without a snake,

musing endlessly on an unpredictable wrath
of nearby Kīlauea or a great typoon
or a hail which may bring the entire island
to sink down into the sea
is to make out what it would be like if I live in Hawaii.

Like the Japanese sudden attack on Pearl Harbour
    during the Pacific War,
I wondered a possible nuclear attack by the Soviet Union.
When I visited the National Memorial Cemetry
and the Diamond military base,
the picture of a mushroom cloud occurred to me
because I pondered over what it would be like
    to take root anew here.

Across the ocean, my home village is to be inundated
under the construction of an industrial dam;

남의 땅 하와이의 시골 마을 지날 때
흰둥이 검둥이 누런둥이 퍼뜨리며
한 삼백년 다시 살 고향 없을까고
좌청룡 우백호를 두루 살핀다.

the blue mountains and family burial grounds would sink down,
and eminent men and human compassion are to be scattered.

Passing by a Hawaiian hamlet in this alien land
and wondering whether I can find a new home
    to live on at least for three hundred years again—
whilst begetting the whites, the blacks, and the yellows,
I look all around the blue dragon on the left
    and the white tiger on the right.

니나

니나, 그 바다 위
선셋 크루즈의 비오는 갑판 위에서
월하향(月下香) 목걸이 걸어주며
물 어린 눈으로 날 쳐다볼 때
정말이지 난 차마 돌아서기 어려웠지

만에 하나 이 배가 갈앉는다면
만원의 구명정에 마지막 한 사람 너를 내리고
난 웃으며 배와 함께 갈앉을 수밖에.
갈앉을 수밖에. . .
아, 정말 그런 그림이 그려지는 순간,

너는 내 귀가를 막는 사이렌? 사이렌?
그래, 난 너를 두고 선실의 춤판에 뛰어들고 말았지
널 피하려, 널 지우려
온몸을 열풍에 찢기운 돛폭처럼 펄럭였지

너는 유람선에서 일하는 사모아 여자
내사 남양의 낙조를 보러 온 두 시간 승객
어쩌란 말이냐,
어쩌란 말이냐
니나라는 이름조차 알 일 없는데. . .

Nina

Nina, on the rainy deck of a sunset cruise
in the sea, when you hanged
a wreath of tuberose around my neck
and looked up at me with your wet eyes,
it was truly difficult for me to turn around.

If this ship sinks down by any chance,
I'd let you get on a jammed lifeboat as a last person.
Then smiling, I myself would go down with the ship
and nothing but go down into the sea . . .
Ah, surely, when such a moment was imagined,

you're a siren blocking my way back home? A siren?
Yea, leaving you alone, I flung myself into
    a dancing party in a cabin
to elude and efface you by fluttering
my whole body like a sailcloth torn by a gale.

You are a deckhand on a cruise from Samoa;
I'm a tourist enjoying a two-hour sunset
    in the South Seas.
What am I supposed to do?
What am I supposed to do?
There is no reason even to know the name, Nina.

근황

몰락하여
돌이킬 수 없는 왕조의
몇 안 되는 신민의
우직한 충정 때문에
눈치보며 살아가는
태자의 팔자처럼.

낡아
쓸모 없는 교조의
눈먼 신봉자의
기분 안 다치려고
억지로 웃음 짓는
집사의 신세처럼.

The Recent Situation

Like an ill-fated crown prince
who lives on his wits
by virtue of the honest loyalty
of few subjects
in the dissolved dynasty
which cannot be undone.

Like the situation of a deacon
who smiles against his will
not to spoil
the mood
of blind followers
who stick to the old, useless creeds.

버드나무

벌판에 외로 솟은
우람한 버드나무
태풍 속의 절규여.

천만 갈래 버들가지
휘저으며 찢기우며
미친 듯 춤 춤이여.

영겁의 사랑
억겁의 저주를
맹세하고 다짐하던

아, 벼락도 천둥도
다스릴 수 없던
젊은 날 내 애증의 모습.

흠뻑 젖은 버드나무
선 채로 이읏고
흐느끼고 있다.

A Willow Tree

An imposing willow tree
soaring up in the lonely field
outcries in a storm.

Ten million twigs
flailed or torn
dance and dance in madness.

Everlasting love
or an eternal curse
was pledged and assured;

ah, that was an image of love-hate
in my youth that even a thunderbolt
or a thunder could not tame.

The willow soaked to the bone
is at last wailing
as in standing.

나르시스

달밤,
호수는 거울이었다.

동굴에서 나온 사내 하나
물가에 엎드렸다.

물을 휘젓곤 들여다보고
또 휘젓곤 또 들여다보고. . .

웃음소리지 울음소린지 몰랐던 것은
휘젓는 물소리 때문이었을까

고개 들어 그가 짐승같이
달을 보고 울었을 때

그때 나는 보았다.
그는 나르시스인 것을

문둥이가 되어 얼굴이 일그러진
나르시스인 것을.

Narcissus[°]

In the moonlit night,
a lake was a mirror.

A man from a cave
leant over the edge of water.

Stirring up the water, he looked into it.
Stirring it up again, he looked into it . . .

Ignorance of whether he was laughing or weeping
was due to the churning sound of the water?

When he held up his head
and howled at the moon like a beast,

at that time, I saw him;
he was a Narcissus.

He was no other than a Narcissus
whose face was contorted as a leper.

° In Greek mythology, Narcissus is name for a beautiful youth who became so entranced with his own reflection in a pool of water. He rejected all romantic advances and fell in love with his own reflection. After his death, a flower bearing his name sprouted in his place.

시골의 달

천지에 그대 설움 달래 줄
아무도 없을 때

여기 냇가에 와
밤하늘 둥근달을 쳐다보아라.

여울에 울먹이는 한 점 돌에도
달빛은 어루만지 듯 내리고 있다.

허영의 거리에서
부나비같이 허둥대다 죽지가 부러진 그대

매연에 그을린 도회의 달이야
피멍 든 속가슴까지 닿을 수 있나

천지에 달 밖엔
그대 보아 줄 아무것도 없을 때

여기 시골에 와
중천에 고운 달과 마주 보아라.

The Rustic Moon

When you have no one
to soothe your sadness,

come here to the banks of a stream
and look up at the round moon in the nightly sky.

Even on a tearful pebble in the rapids,
the moonlight descends caressingly.

You are like a tiger moth whose shoulder blade
    is broken,
whilst fluttering in the street of vanity.

How can the urban moon smeared with smoke
reach a deeply scarred inner heart?

When there is no one in the world
to see you save the moon,

come here to the countryside
and behold the lovely moon amidst the sky.

달맞이꽃

달을 보러
냇가에 나갔다.

노오란 달맞이꽃들이
환하게 피어 있었다.

나만 달을
좋아하는 줄 알았는데

저들은 뭣 땜에
달을 처다보는가

달도 밤이슬로 반짝이는 꽃들 위에
마냥 달빛을 쏘고 있지 않는가,

문득, 나는 안중에도 없는 듯해
서운하였다.

A Sundrops

To look up at the moon,
I went out to the banks of a stream.

Golden sundrops
were fully abloom.

I reckoned there were none
who loved the moon save me.

What did they look up
at the moon for?

The moon was ever shedding its light
on them gleaming in the evening dew!

Since they seemed not to give a toss,
suddenly, I felt sad.

영구(靈柩) 앞에서

이젠 턱도 혀도 굳어졌으니
사랑이여,
배고픔도 더는 그댈
성가시진 못하겠지.

꺼이꺼이
산 사람은 길게 울다가
눈물 닦고 돌아앉아
밥을 먹는다.

Before a Coffin

Now that your jaw and tongue got stiff,
love,
even hunger may not bother you
any longer.

Wailing with sobs,
the survivor weeps himself out.
Drying his tears, he rolls over
and eats a meal.

종언(終焉)

사랑이여,

허허벌판에
자욱하게 내려 쌓이는 눈발 속에서
걸인 내외가 불어 피우는
화톳불이여.

무녀(巫女)의 몸짓같이
연기만 오르고
찔레 붉은 열매만한 불꽃 한 점
피어나지 않는 것을, 피어나지 않는 것을,

나는 차마 너의 탓이라고
너는 설마 나의 탓이라고
속눈 흘기지나 않나
못 미더워 않나 의심할 때는

천축(天竺)의 길 이야기보다 가슴 설레고
저 푸르디푸른 세월을 탕진하여
빚어낸 고려청자
그 수련한 태깔의 우리 사랑은

Desition

Love,

in the empty wildness
amidst the flurry of thickly piling snow,
there was a bonfire made by the puffing
of a beggary husband and wife.

Like the movement of a shaman,
smoke rises up only;
a speck of flame as small as the red fruit
of a briar will not rise and not ever.

I cannot even say, *You are blamable*:
you may not say, *I am blamable.*
When we look askance at each other
or doubt about distrustfulness,

our love,
more throbbing than a travelogue to India
or a fine form and colour like a Goryeo celadon°
made by consuming those days of azure blue,

무엇이 되느냔 말이야!

what would it become of!

° A Goryeo celadon was chiefly made during the Goryeo dynasty between 918 and 1392. It is highly regarded as one of world cultural treasures. A celadon is a type of jade-green porcelain. Production of this type of ceramic ware reached its height during the Goryeo dynasty. So, it is commonly referred to as a Goryeo celadon.

라일락

정원 한쪽의
라일락 그늘에 서서
그녀는 화안히 웃고 있었다.

나는 반가웠으나
휠체어에 앉아서
그녀를 향해
쓸쓸히 웃어 주었다.

내게로 다가올 때
웨이브 진 머릿결이
옛날처럼 나부끼고

손길이
내 이마에
꽃향기로 얹히더니,

시야엔
다시
라일락 꽃더미 뿐.

Lilacs

Standing in the shady nook
of lilacs in the garden,
she was all smiles.

I was glad to see her,
but stuck to a wheelchair.
I smiled at her
forlornly.

When she came over to me,
her wavy hair
flapped as it used to,

her hand
was laid on my forehead
as if a floral scent.

In sight
again,
there was only a pile of lilacs.

그때 나는 내 속에서
남몰래 울고 있던 한 사내의
울음의 끝부분을 듣고 있었다.

At that time, I was listening to
the end of a man's secret crying
within me.

나의 청춘 마리안느

—옛날 영화

조조할인
송국 극장 객석엔
나 혼자뿐이었다.
줄리앙 듀비비에의
'나의 청춘 마리안느'
저녁에 보러 갔어도
나 혼자뿐이었다.

썰렁한 극장 안 낡은 스크린
그르그르 소리를 내며 영사기가 돌았다.
폭풍 불고 번개 치는 밤, 소년은
나체로 다가선 여자를 뿌리치고
안개 낀 고성에 감금된
운명의 여자 마리안느를 구해 내고 있었다.

배우의 이름도
마지막 장면도 분명하지 않지만
필시 이루지 못한 사랑의 이야기였다,
소년이 결연히 말하고 있었다.
'안드로메다까지라도 찾아갈 거야'.'

Marianne de ma jeunesse°

—An old movie

Early morning discount.
There was no one
in Songguk movie theatre but me.
Marianne de ma jeunesse
directed by Julien Duvivier.
When I went there in the evening,
none was there but me, too.

In the chilly theatre, the screen was shabby
and the bioscope was purring.
In a stormy and lightning night,
turning down the lure of a naked woman,
a boy was rescuing the fateful lady,
Marianne, captured in the misty old castle.

Although the names of actors
and the last scene are not also clear,
it must be the story of a hopeless love.
Resolutely, the boy was speaking;
I will go to find her to Andromeda.

That night, I wrote an anonymous letter

그날 밤 나는 내 짝사랑에게
익명의 편지 한 통을 보냈지.
'안드로메다라도 찾아 갈 거야
나의 청춘 마리안느.'

to my unrequited lover.

I will go to find you even to Andromeda,

Marianne of my youth.

° *Marianne de ma jeunesse* ("Marianne of My Youth") is a 1955 French-West German romantic movie directed by Julien Duvivier. It is based on a 1932 novel *Schmerzliches Arkadien* by Peter von Mendelssohn.

오십 년 후

중학생 때 그녀 할머니 처음 뵈었을 때
난 왜 그런 생각 했을까
흰옷에 하얀 머리 비녀 지르시고
봄 햇볕 쪼이러 마루에 나앉은
검버섯에 주름 많던 그녀 할머니
누나야, 내 짝사랑 너도 늙으면
쪼글쪼글 너네 할머니 모습일거라고.

오늘 아침 우연히 신문 보고 알았다며
오십 년 만에 처음 전화하는 너
나는 쿵쿵대는 가슴을 진정하며
어쩔 줄 몰라 한다는 말이
요즘도 옛날 모습 지니고 있냐니까
염색머리, 틀니에 보청기까지 쓰는
영 틀려버린 할망구란다.

그래, 누나야 너도 죽으면
너네 할머니 닮은 해골 되겠지
그땐 나도 내 무덤 속 전화도 없는 곳에서
백골로 누워 가끔은 네가 궁금하겠지
생각밖에 할 것 없는 긴 긴 시간 속에서

After Fifty Years

When I was a secondarian and first saw her grandma,
why did I ever think in that way?
In white clothes and white hair with a pin,
basking in the spring sun on the wooden floor,
her granny was full of age spots and winkles.
Older sister, my crush, when you get old,
you will be like your winkled grandma as well.

Saying she happened to know through the paper
    this morning,
she gave me a ring first in fifty years.
Calming down my throbbing heart,
what I blurted out all in a fluster was
    whether she has kept an old look.
Dyeing her hair black with dentures and a hearing aid—
she said bluntly, *A hopeless hag.*

Yea, dear sister, when you are dead,
you'll also turn to a skeleton like your granny.
At that time, I'll also lie supine as a skeleton
in my grave where there is no phone-call.

더러는 네 백골이 떠오르겠지.
열다섯 그때 얼굴 떠오르겠지.

At times, I'll wonder about you at the place
where there is nothing but musing in a long, long hour.
At times, your white skeleton may come across my mind,
    and your face at fifteen as well.

내 아직 적막에 길들지 못해

미닫이에 푸른 달빛
날 놀라게 해

일어나 빈 방에
좌불처럼 앉다.

내 아직 적막에
길들지 못해

버레소리 잦아지는
시오 리 밤길

달 아래 그대 문 앞
다다름이여.

울 넘어 꽃내음만
한참 맡다가

I'm Not Acquainted Yet with Quiescence

Since the blue moonlight
on a sliding door startles me,

I get up in a vacant room
and sit like a seated Buddha.

For I'm not acquainted yet
with quiescence,

A nightly tramp at fifteen-ri°
where insects' chirping gets louder—

I have nearly arrived at the gate
of your house under the moon.

After smelling flowers for a while
planted inside the hedgerow,

° Ri is a Korean traditional unit of measuring a distance. Ten ri is equivalent to 4km.

달 흐르는 여울길
돌아오나니

내 아직 적막,
길들지 못해.

I come home across the rapids
in the gleaming moonlght.

I'm not acquainted yet
with quiescence.

운산동 광인(狂人) 내외

집 앞 행길에 버스가 서면
그녀는 가겠다는 듯이
영 아주 떠나겠다는 듯이 달려 나왔다.

집 앞 행길에 버스가 서면
사내는 달려 나와 그녀 뒤에 붙어 섰다.

그녀는 한 번도 차에 오르지 않았다.
사내는 한 번도 말리지 않았다.

행길에 버스가 서면 그녀는 달려 나오고
그녀가 나서면 사내는 따라 나오지만,

차는 이윽고 가버리고
그들은 싱긋 웃으며 돌아오는 것이었다.

차를 기다리는 것은
도시 그 재미 때문이었다.

A Crazy Couple at Unsandong

When a bus drew up on the road
    before the house,
she rushed out of her abode
as if departing for good.

When a bus stopped along the road
    before the house,
her man stormed out of the house
    and stood close behind her.

She has never got on the bus;
her man has never told her not to.

Whenever a bus stops on the road,
    she runs out of her house
and her man runs after her.

At last, the bus pulls away;
flashing a smile, they turn back.

Waiting for a bus itself
was the only reason for fun.

3부
Part Three

색실

어린 아기 적 나는 어여쁜 색실 한 파람을
가지고 놀다가 그만 몹시 헝클고 말았습니다.
나는 온종일 그걸 풀어 보려고 애썼지만
끝내 풀 수가 없어 엉엉 울어버렸습니다.
어머닌, 까짓것, 하찮은 거라며 버리게 하고
보다 예쁘고 긴 색실을 주셨습니다.
나는 울음을 그치긴 했지만 풀다 버린
그 색실이 몹시 아까웠습니다.

나는 자라면서 더욱 아름다운 형형색색의
수 많은 색실을 보았습니다.
나는 그들 중 얼마나 많은 것을
또 헝클었는지 모릅니다.
그걸 풀려고 얼마나 많은 세월을
허비했는지 모릅니다.
그걸 풀지 못하고 버리면서
얼마나 아까와했는지 모릅니다.

색실은 내가 자라 청년이 되어 갈수록
질기고 길어져
풀기는 커녕 때론 내 손을 감고 몸을 감아

Coloured Threads

When I was a toddler, I played with
a skein of thread but messed it up.
I tried to unravel all day long
but failed to the end. So, I bawled.
Mom, saying, "Well, no problem,
    let me throw it away",
gave me a far prettier, longer thread.
Though I stopped crying, it was such a waste
to throw out the coloured thread.

As I grew up, I have seen lots of skeins
of coloured, prettier threads.
I have no idea how many of them
I messed up again,
and how many days I have spent
trying to unravel them.
After throwing the unravelled thread out,
I don't know how often I have grudged.

When I grew into a youth, the coloured
thread turned tenacious and longer.

헤어나지 못할 뻔한 일조차 있었으니까요.
어른이 된 지금에사 돌이켜 보니
인생은 색실을 헝클곤 풀다가 버리고,
또 헝클곤 풀다가 버리는 짓의
연속이 아닌가 싶습니다.

앞으로 또 몇 파람의 색실이
내 앞에 놓여질지 모르지만
아, 나라는 사람은 그걸 또 만질 것인지
그냥 둘 것인지 아직도 전혀
짐작할 수가 없습니다.

Far from being unravelled,
it coiled up around my hands and body,
and once I almost couldn't get out of it.
Looking back now as a grown-up,
I think life is but a succession of ravelling
or unravelling or discarding the coloured thread.

I have no idea how many skeins of
coloured thread lie ahead of me, though.
Ah, a man who I am
can't guess at all yet
whether I will touch it or leave it again.

용계(龍溪) 은행나무

이것은
선 채로 흘러가는
유유한 장강(長江)

웅대한 코러스
포르테씨씨모의 환희

이것은
법열로 가득 찬
오도(悟道)의 현장.

천 년 가람(伽藍)
설법하는 큰 스님.

영원이란 걸
잘 생각해 보라시며
은행잎 하나 던져 주시다.

A Ginkgo Tree at Yonggye°

This
is a long river running slowly,
as if unmoving.

A grand chorus:
a glee of fortissississimo.

This
is a venue of awakening
filled with a mystical rapture.

One-thousand-year old Buddhist temple;
a sermonizing monk of great renown.

Letting me mull over
eternity,
it casts a leaf of ginkgo.

° Yonggye ginkgo tree is known to be as old as 700 years. It is designated as natural monument No. 175. It is located at Yonggyeo-ri, Giran-myeon, Andong city.

취운정(翠雲亭) 마담에게

굳이
어느 새벽꿈 속에서나마
나 만난 듯하다는
그대.

내 열 번 전생의
어느 가을볕 잔잔한 한나절을
각간(角干) 유신(庾信)의 집 마당귀에
엎드려 여물 씹는 소였을 적에

등허리에
살짝
앉았다 떠난
까치였기나 하오.

참
그날
쪽같이 푸르던
하늘빛이라니.

To a Madam at Chwiunjeong

It was you who said
once for all
that you seemed to have seen me
in an early morning dream.

Perhaps in my tenth reincarnation
when I was an ox chewing fodder at the corner
of the courtyard in Kim Yu-sin's° residence
for half a day in the placid autumnal sun,

you might have been a magpie
alighted
furtively
on my back and have flown off.

Aha,
on the day,
the sky was
as blue as indigo.

° Kim Yu-sin (595-673) was a military general and statesman from Silla kingdom, who had played a central role in unifying ancient three kingdoms in the Korean peninsular by defeating Baekje and Goguryeo. He was the highest ranking official during King Muyeol, who unified and reigned the unified Silla kingdom between 654 and 661.

공작수(孔雀愁)

그대, 인도 옛 왕조의 어느 호사하던 왕,

머리에 조촐한 화관을 이고
깃털의 송이송이 들꽃 다발을
누구를 송축하여 이따금 펼쳐 보이나.

칠보(七寶)의 구중궁(九重宮)
무녀(舞女)의 나른한 팔에 감기어
환락이 천국마냥 지겹던 사내
전쟁과 패륜으로 지루를 달래던 왕,

잡아온 토인 미녀의
몸을 탐내다가
마음을 빼앗기고
눈물 배워 마침내
착하고 겁 많은 임금으로 살다가

그녀 죽자 그대 또한 슬픔으로 숨져
온몸에 비애의 푸른 멍을 띠고
이승에 한 마리 공작으로 태어난
그대 인도 옛 왕조의 눈물 많던 왕,

Peacock's Anxiety

You were an opulent king
    in an ancient Indian kingdom.

Crowned with a simple coronet on your head,
who do you eulogize now and then by spreading out
a bouquet of wild flowers on your plumage?

In a palace adorned with seven treasures,
cuddled by the languid arms of a dancing girl,
you were a man who got bored with pleasure
    as much as in heaven;
you were a king who was soothing ennui
    with a war and depravity.

Desiring the body of an aboriginal beauty
captured from expedition,
you lost your heart to her
but learned tears.
At last, you lived as an honest, timid king.

When she died, you also died of grief.
With bluish bruises all over your body,

깃털엔
수백 수천의 호동그란 눈을 쳐들고
누굴 찾아
이따금 사위(四圍)를 살피나.

you were a tearful king reincarnated
    into a peacock in this world
from the kingdom of ancient India.

Lifting a myriad of startled eyes
from your plumage,
whom are you looking for
by keeping a sharp lookout now and then?

커튼콜

막이 내렸지만
브라보를 외쳐 대는 객석의
열띤 환호에 답하여
여러 차례 무대에 나서는
배우나 가수는 멋있다.

지금은 가고 없는 위인들 중에도
두고두고 우리를 감동케 하여
새록새록 떠오르는 이름들이 있다.
백 년 또는 천 년도 더 전의 역사의 무대에 섰던 이들을
우리는 다시 기려 추모하는 것 아닌가

참으로 값진 것은
오늘 열 번의 커튼콜보다도
천 년이나 만 년 후 사람들의 기억의 커튼을 젖히고
꿈속의 얼굴처럼 떠오르는 일이다.
구름 속의 달처럼 내비치는 것이다.

아, 우리는 어쩌면 우리의 무대를 떠나서도
머언 먼 미래의 사람들의 머릿속에, 가슴속에
친구처럼 연인처럼 떠오를 수 있을까

A Curtain Call

After a curtain falls,
it looks nice for an actor or a singer
to return to a stage again and again
to take a curtain call
from the audience yelling bravo.

Among great people who are gone now,
there are names that pop up again and again,
and touch our heart for a long time.
That is why we pay tribute to historical figures
who lived one hundred or thousand years ago.

What is a real worth—more than ten times—of today's
curtain calls, is to draw a curtain of memory
for those who will come up one thousand
    or ten thousands years later,
and to enter their mind like a visage in a dream;
it's like a moonbeam breaking rifted clouds.

Ah, after we depart from our stage,
how can we make latercomers recall us as a friend
or a lover in their head or heart in the remote future?

오늘 빌린 옛날 비디오에 나와서
나를 울리는,
사라진 영웅들의
한창 때 모습처럼.

Just like old heroes in their heyday
who made me cry
by appearing in the old videos
that I borrowed today.

내 아내

나는 만약 다시 태어난다면
여자가 되어야겠다고 하니
아내는 다시 태어나면
남자가 되겠단다.

나는 여자로 태어나 당신 같은 남편을 만나
시중을 좀 더 잘 들겠다고 하니
아내는 남자로 태어나 나를 들볶고
구박해 보았으면 원이 없겠단다.

나는 들볶이고 구박을 받으면서도
남편을 위해 잘 참고 견디겠다 하니
아내는 내가 아무리 잘해 줘도
한사코 트집 잡고 윽박질러 볼 거라 한다.

아내여
갈쿠리 손에 흰 머리칼 듬성한
미운 아내여

어디 내생에 다시 나더라도
멀리 가지나 마오.

My Wife

If I were born again,
I said, I should be a woman.
If she were born again,
my wife retorted, she would be a man.

Born as a woman, I would have a husband
like you and wait on you hand and foot, I said.
My wife riposted, if she were born as a man,
there would be nothing more desirable than
    hassling and harnessing me.

Even if I were hassled and harnessed,
I replied, I should bear and forbear for my husband.
Even if I would do my best for my husband,
she hurled back, adamantly she would cavil
    and browbeat.

My daring,
my homely wife whose hands are
like a rake and whose gray hair is thin—

even if you were born again,
don't go off from me, please.

개안(開眼)

무량수불전(無量壽佛殿) 앞 댓돌 밑에
눈 비비며 기어 나온 꽃뱀 한 마리,
몇 겁(劫) 후면 보살(菩薩)로나 태어날거나
무심힌 듯 법당(法堂) 안을 쳐다보고 있네.

Enlightenment

Below the front terrace stones of the Amitabha Hall,
rubbing its eyes, a tiger snake crawls out.
After some kalpas, it may be reborn as a Bodhisattva;
attentively, it looks up into the Buddha Hall.

산중대작(山中對酌)

별빛 쏟아지는 마당에
평상을 펴고

개다리소반을 마주해
친구와 쉬엄쉬엄
차를 마신다.

아내는
마른 쑥으로
모깃불을 피우며

서울 친구의
신기한 세상 얘길
홀린 듯 엿듣는다.

뒷산 소쩍새가
휘영청
달무리를 흔들자

손님은
그만 이야길 멈춘다.

Hob or Nob in the Mountains

After bringing a low wooden bench
to the courtyard at a glittering starry night

and sitting face to face with a crony
at a small dining table with cabrioles,
I have tea with him off and on.

My wife
is making a mosquito fire
with dried mugwort,

whilst listening in on a marvelous story
told by my friend from Seoul,
as if bewitched.

When a cuckoo on the hill
behind the house
shakes a bright lunar halo,

my guest
stops talking.

백 번을 들어도 싫지 않는 새소리
백 번을 들어도 야릇한 세상사.

친구여. 날 밝거든
냇가에 나가
멍텅구리 낚시나 담그어 보세.

It's not unpleasing to hear the birdsong
    as many times as a hundred;
yet, the ways of world sound odd to hear
    as many times as a hundred.

My dear chum, when day breaks,
let's go to the stream
to fish by angling.

딱따구리

아침에 문득 뒷산에서
다르르르르
다르르르르
문풍지 떠는 소리가 난다.

아, 저건 딱따구리 아닌가
맹랑한 놈
얼마나 강한 부리를 가졌기에
착암기처럼 나무를 쪼아
벌레를 꺼내 먹는단 말인가

아직 눈바람이 찬데
벌레들이 기지개 켜며
하품 소리라도 냈단 말인가.

옛사람은 무얼로
벼룻물이 어는 이 추위 속에
봄이 와 있는 걸 알았을까

감고을축입춘(敢告乙丑立春)이라 써서
사당 문에 붙이는데

A Woodpecker

Suddenly in the morning from the hill
    at the back of my house—
Da-r-r-r-r
Da-r-r-r-r—
the sound of a vibrating weather strip is heard.

Ah, that isn't a woodpecker?
It's really something—
like a rock drill, how strong beak
does it have to forage insects
by pecking at the tree?

A snow-chilled wind still blows.
I wonder whether stretching insects
have let out yawning.

How did ancient men know that spring has already come
in such cold
that makes water for an inkstone freezing?

When *Greetings on the Onset of Spring in the Year of Ox* is posted on the door of a shrine—

다르르르르 다르르르르
뒷산에선 그예
문풍지 떠는 소리가 난다.

Da-r-r-r-r, Da-r-r-r-r—
on the hill at the back of the house,
assuredly, the vibration of a weather strip resonates.

칩거

절 마루에 산새가 와서 울어
유마경(維摩經) 읽다 말고 귀 기울이네.
문살에 어른대는 자목련 망울 고와도
산새 쫓을까 문을 못 열어.

예불 온 손님들 기침소리 나는데
나아가 맞으려도 봄 햇볕 눈부실가
닳아진 책지 같은 문짝만
바라다가 또 바라보다가.

A Life in Seclusion

When a mountain bird alights on the wooden
floor of a temple and chirps,
I stop reading Vimalakirti Sutra° and listen to it.
Though the buds of a lily magnolia wavering
on the paper sliding door are lovely,
I cannot open the door from fear to drive
the bird away.

A dry cough is heard from guests who came
to offer a prayer chanting, though,
I don't feel like greeting them, for I may go blind
by the sunbeams of springtime. I gaze and gaze
at the door, just like the worn-out poor paper.

° It is a Mahayana Buddhist Sutra. Perhaps it may date from no later than the third century A.D. It is a combination of stories and theoretical teachings that can counteract mental afflictions in the meditator.

학(鶴)

푸른 산을 가로질러
학이 날고 있다.

어디서 와서
어디로 가나.

천지간을 오르내리고
유명(幽明) 간을 드나드는 혼이여.

문득 보였다간
흔적 없이 사라지는 새.

지금 저기 물가에
적요히 쉬고 있다.

A Crane

Across the blue mountains,
a crane flies.

From where it comes
and whither it goes, I wonder.

Going up and down
    between heaven and earth,
it is a spirit going in and out
    between this and that world.

It is such a bird that turns up at once
and vanishes away into thin air.

Now it rests over there in quietude
by the shore of a stream.

여울을 베고 누워

밤 강물에 멱을 감기는
유월 보름이 제일이라.

사람들은 마을을 비우고
여울을 베고 누웠다.

암만 오래 있어도
춥잖고 덥지 않은
어머니 품속같이 아늑한 물속

머리만 내밀어 돌을 베고 누워
물소릴 자장가 삼아
잠을 청해 보기도 한다.

낙원이 어떤 건지 알고 싶거든
삼굿하는 유월 보름 낮을 보내고
밤 되어 달빛 아래 여울에 들 일이다.

Pillowing on the Rapids

There is nothing like the sixth full moon
of the lunar year for bathing in a river.

The village folk vacate their homes
and lie down by pillowing on the rapids.

However long one stays in water,
it is neither chilly nor warm;
it is as snug as in mom's arms.

Sticking his head out of water, he lies down
by pillowing his head on the stone in the rapids
and tries to sleep while listening to babbling,
    as if it were a lullaby.

If one wants to know what a paradise is like,
after spending the daytime at hemp-steaming,
he should lie down in the moonlit rapids
    on the night of the sixth lunar full moon.

개구리 소리

해마다 고운 연꽃 가까이서 보려고
앞마당에 연 단지 갖다 놨더니
밤마다 청개구리, 무당개구리 모여들어
시끄럽게 우는구나, 줄기차게 우는구나.

개구리의 합창은 자연의 소리
부르고 화답하고 함께 부르는 사랑의 노래
그러나 교향곡도 밤마다 들으면 지겨운 법
그것도 같은 곡만 들으면 괴로운 법.

드디어 난 연 단지를 담 밖으로 옮겨버렸다.
낮에는 길 가는 이가 꽃 보고 좋아하고
밤이면 멀리서 들리는 음악회 소리.
버리면 맘 편해지는 법, 새삼 깨닫네.

The Croaking of Frogs

Since I brought a lotus pot to the front courtyard
to take a closer look at its flowers every year,
the green, red-bellied frogs flock together
    every evening
and croak noisily without cease.

A chorus of frogs is the sound of nature:
it is a song of love in chorus by singing
    and responding to it.
Yet if one hears a symphony every night,
    it makes him get bored.
If one hears the same tune again and again,
    it makes him distressed.

At last, I removed the pot over the wall;
in daytime, pedestrians relish the flowers
and at night, croaking is like a music concert
    from a distance.
Again, I realize renouncing sets one's mind at ease.

집 보는 날

대문 밖에 인기척이 나서
내다보니
저녁 햇살을 지고
거지 사내가 지나간다.

제가 커피를요?
놀림을 당하는 기분이 들까
지전(紙錢) 한 장을 미리 주었다.

컵을 쥔 손이 수전증으로 떨고 있었지만
몸을 깨끗이 하고 있었다면
술도 한 잔 했을 것을. . .

전화도 배달부도 오지 않는
적막한 오후
아내는 외출하고
나 홀로 집 보는 날.

두 뼘 남은 해를 지고
사내도 가 버리고. . .

On a Day When I Look After a House

Outside the main gate, someone is around;
I look out.
Carrying an evening glow on his back,
a begger is passing by.

"Coffee for me?", he asks awkwardly.
Not let him feel teased,
I gave him a banknote in advance.

His hand holding the cup was shaking
    due to a hand tremor,
but if he was clean,
I might have a drink with him . . .

It was a lonely afternoon
with neither a phone-call nor a postman.
It was the day when my wife went out
and I was alone looking after the house.

Carrying the sun—left over two spans
    before sundown—on his back,
the man is gone, too . . .

멧돼지야 나오너라

우리 집 음식 쓰레기 어김없이 먹어 주는
기특한 멧돼지
일 년 내 따러 먹고 쏟아부은 매실주 건덕지를
흔적 없이 먹어치우고는
사흘 째 종무소식.
쓰레기는 쌓이는데,
너무 오래 자고 있는 거 아닌가?

Come out, the Wild Boar

It is an admirable boar
because it eats up unfailingly
all of the leftover from my house.
After devouring the dregs out of
    plum wine consumed all year round,
it did not show up for three days.
The leftover is piled up—
Isn't it sleeping too long?, I wonder.

호숫가 오솔길

가보자
굴참나무 검은 둥치와
미풍에 사운대는 나뭇잎 사이로
은비늘 반짝이는 호수를 보러.

호숫가 오솔길은 낙엽에 덮여 있고
낙엽을 밟으며
키 큰 나무 그늘 속을 걸어 가보자.
호수를 바라보며 걸어 가보자.

아침이면 물안개 하얗게 피고
달밤이면 금물결 반짝이는 곳
호숫가 오솔길을 걸어 가보자.
쉬엄쉬엄 숲길 따라 걸어 가보자.

때로는 호수 위로 소나기가 지나가고
때로는 적막강산 눈 내리는 것 보러
키 큰 나무 그늘 속을 걸어 가보자.
호숫가 오솔길을 걸어 가보자.

A Footpath by the Lake

Let us go
to watch the lake glittering like a silver scale
betwixt the black trunks of oriental oak trees
and their whiffling leaves in the breeze.

The lakeside trail is covered with fallen leaves.
Treading on dead leaves,
let us walk in the shade of tall trees.
Looking across the lake, let us walk along.

This is where a white wet fog rises over the lake
    in the morning
and golden ripples glitter in the moonlit night.
Let us walk along the footpath by the lake.
Let us walk off and on along a woodland path.

At times, let us walk in the shade of tall trees
to watch a shower crossing the lake
and at times snow falling in dead quietness.
Let us walk along the woodland path.

4부
Part Four

걷고 싶은 길

숲길을 걷고 싶다.
쭉쭉 곧고
굵게 자란 나무
숲 사이로 난
황톳길을 걷고 싶다.
햇살 받아
반들거리는 초록 잎
향기 뿜는 꽃숭어리 사이로
뻐꾸기 소리 들으며 매미 소리 들으며
하루에 한 오십 리 걷고 싶구나.
하루에 걸어서 시골길 오십 리를 가면
거기 자그만 마을에 민박집 있고,
차편에 보낸 짐을 끌러 옷 갈아입고
마을 축제장이나 야시장 같은 델
어슬렁거려도 보고,
이튿날도 걸어서
숲속 길 또 오십 리를 가면
아궁이에 발갛게 장작이 타는 농가가 있고
토벽 냄새나는 사랑방 따뜻한 아랫목에서
도토리묵에 시원한 막걸리도 얻어 마시고
또 일어나 걸어서 산속 길 오십 리를 가면

A Footpath I'd Like to Walk Along

I'd like to walk along a woodland path.
Through the thick-grown grove of
straight and upright trunks,
I'd like to walk along
a red clay path.
Amidst green leaves lustrous in sunlight
and the clusters of fragrant flowers
while listening to a cuckoo and a cicada,
I'd like to walk about fifty-ri in a day.
If I walk about fifty-ri in the countryside,
I may find a bed and breakfast in a hamlet.
Changing clothes out of the package
    sent earlier by a car,
I may saunter around a village fête
or a night fair.
Next day, if I walk in the distance
of fifty-ri again along a woodland path,
I may come across a farmhouse
    with a firewood burning in the furnace,
and be invited to a warm spot nearest
    to the furnace in a man's guest room

풍경소리, 목탁소리
향불 냄새 나는 산사가 있고
야삼경 구성진 염불소리
잠결엔 듯 꿈결엔 듯 듣기도 하고. . .
콘크리트도 아스팔트도 찻길도 아닌 길
산꿩이 날고 다람쥐며 노루가 다니는 도보 길을
풀을 밟으며 낙엽을 밟으며
때로는 이웃들과, 더러는 아이 손잡고
노래하며 얘기하며 걸었으면 좋겠다.
길에서 만난 사람들과
헤어졌다 또 만나며
한가로이
한가로이
걸어서 갈 수 있는
숲에서 숲으로 이어진
시원한 길을 만들자.
맑은 물과 푸른 바람이 흐르는 숲에
걷기 좋은 길을 만들자.
때로는 동쪽으로 동해 바다까지
때로는 서쪽으로 서해 바다까지
남해까지 그리고 백두까지

walled by the smelly mud and treated with
acorn jelly and fresh *makgeolli*.
If I walk along fifty-ri again after getting up,
I may hear wind-bells tinkling or wooden-bells
ringing from a Buddhist temple
lurked in incence smell on the mountains
or an enchanting Buddhist prayer at the dead of night,
as if in a sleep or in a dream . . .
Neither a concrete roadway nor an asphalt,
but a trail over which a pheasant flies
or a squirrel and a roe deer haunt around is
where I like to walk on the grass or the fallen leaves.
At times, I'd like to walk with other pedestrians
or at times with children in singing and talking
hand in hand.
Meeting again with the pedestrians
from whom we parted on the way—
leisurely
and leisurely,
let us make a footpath which links
one woodland to another;

곧고 굵게 자란 나무숲 속, 걸을 수 있는 길이
끝없이 이어지고 또 이어져 있으면 좋겠다.

a refreshing path.
In the woodland where clean water runs
  and a fresh wind blows,
let us make a pedestrian-friendly path,
sometimes which leads to the East Sea,
sometimes to the Yellow Sea from the west,
to the southern sea and up to Mt. Baekdu.
It would be wonderful if a footpath is linked
  to another in the grove made of straight
and upright trees without end.

상모재

달 아래
눈 위에
그림자 하나

밤길 혼자서
재 넘어간다.

열두 발 휘날리는
상모 같은 길에

언뜻 사라졌다
다시 보이는

아득히 흔들리며
가는 점 하나.

밤길 나 혼자
재 넘어 간다.

Sangmojae Pass

Under the moonlight,
a shadow
on the snow.

At night, I am going alone
over a mountain pass.

Along the pass like a twelve-bal°-length
twirling ribbon tied to sangmo°°,

all of a sudden, he is out of sight
and then in sight.

Swaying dimly,
a speck is moving.

At night, I am going alone
over a mountain pass.

° A traditional unit of measuring a distance between a fingertip point to another fingertip point in outstetched arms.

°° A bunch of red tassels attached to the top of a hat worn by the farmers when they perform the traditional Korean farmers' dance.

울향(鬱香)

장날 아침
장바닥에
영감님이 전을 폈다.
이건 한석봉 천자문
저건 명심보감.
철 늦은 토정비결
청랑결도 보이고
병진년 대한민력도 보인다.
붓 서너 자루
벼루 두어 개
먹 토막도 놓인 옆에
호박씨
수박씨
물외씨
상추씨
시금치며
월동초며
팝씨 통도 늘어놓고,

우수와
경칩 사이
봄비 오다 개인 오늘

Ulleungdo Juniper

In the morning of a market day,
an old pedlar displayed his merchandise
in the marketplace.
This is a book of *Cheonjamun*° by Seok-bong Han
and that is *Myungsimbogam*°°.
There are also the belated *Tojeong Bigyeol*°°°,
Cheongranggyeol°°°° and *Korean Almanac*
in the year of byeongjin°°°°°.
Three or four writing brushes
and a couple of inkstones are in sight.
Beside a piece of inkstick,
the seeds of pumpkin,
watermelon,
water cucumber,

° *Cheonjamun* (千字文), *The Thousand-Character Text*, was a preliminary text for studying Chinese classics. A primier of Chinese chacracters is known orignially written in the 6th century in China. It was challigraphed by Han Ho (1543-1605), whose art name is Seok Bong in the middle of the Joseon dynasty.

°° *Myungsimbogam* is a book of wise sayings from the ancient Chinese classics and noted sages compiled by Chujeok (1246-1317), during the regin of King Chungryeol in the Goryeo dynasty.

°°° An old form of fortune telling. *The Tojeong Bigyeol* was written by Yi Ji-ham (1517-1578), whose art name is Tojeong.

°°°° A concise summary of *Donguiboham*, a famous book of oriental medicine written by Heo Jun (1517-1578) during the reign of King Gwanghae in 1610.

°°°°° The year of byeongjin is the 53rd year of the sexagenary cycle.

석 자 넉 자 목판 앞에
햇볕만 쬐고 있다.
찬칼
짝재칼도
가지런히 놓인 중에
엄지만한
나무토막이 있어
뭐냐니까
울향이란다.

lettuce,
spinach,
rape,
and a box of beans are displayed.
Between *usu*
and *gyeongchip*[○○○○○○],
spring rain had come
and stopped today.
Before a small wooden box,
the pedlar is just basking in the sun.
I saw a piece of wood
as big as a thumb
among a kitchen knife
and a jack knife
orderly displayed.
I asked, *What is that piece?*
His answer was *Ulhyang*[○○○○○○○].
Snuffing it,

○○○○○○ One of the 24 seasons by the lunar calendar that falls around the 19th of February. Usually, winter gives way to spring around this time. *Gyeongchip* comes around the 5th of March on the solar calendar, and the coming of *Gyeongchip* implies the end of hibernation.

○○○○○○○ "Ulhyang" is a short form of Ulleung-do juniper tree. It is designated as a natural monument. The folk woodcraft made of Ulleung-do juniper is famous for its pattern and fragrance.

코에 대고
냄샐 맡으며
정말 울향이냐니까
코에 대고 냄샐 맡으며
정말이란다.
저기 참빗
얼레빗
찰고뭇줄 파는 젊은이가 울릉도서 가져온 거라 했다.
오십 원 주고 하나 샀다.

I asked back, *Whether it is real ulhyang?*
Snuffing it on his part,
the old man replied, *it is real ulhyang.*
He said, *the man who sells fine-tooth combs,*
wide-tooth combs and rubber-bands over there
has brought them from Ulleung-do.
I purchased the piece for 50 won.

삼경(三更)

대웅보전 뒷산에 와
우는 소쩍새

엊그제 머리 깎은
총각 중 울리려고

서러이 사러이
울음 우는데

법당 안 조는 부처
그걸 모르고

울지마라 울지마라
울지 마라며

온밤 내 소쩍새만
달래고 있다.

At the Dead of Night

A calling cuckoo on the hill
behind the daeungbojeon°,

as if it would bring tears to an acolyte
whose hair was cut a couple days ago.

It is bawling
sadly and sadly.

The Buddha dozing in his hall
is unaware of it;

he says simply,
Don't cry, don't cry, don't cry,

and coaxes the cuckoo only
all night long.

° A main building in a temple in which the statues of Buddhas and Bodhisattvas are enshrined.

월석(月石)

-스미소니언 박물관에서

이 새까맣고 단단한 것이
다이아나의 살결이란 말인가
떨리는 손가락을
돌에 대어 본다.

돌이여,
사십오 억년 전에 지구를 떠났다는 달에서
고향에 돌아온 돌이여,

널 데려 온 아폴로도
네 옆에 의젓이 쉬고 있구나.

마침 유리창 밖에서
둥근 달이 기웃거리기에

보고 지나가라고
비켜 서 주었다.

Moonrock

—At the Smithsonian Museum

What a pitch-black, hard thing—
is this the texture of Diana's skin°?
I touched it
with my trembling fingers.

Oh, the rock!
It came back home from the moon
after departing from the earth 45 billion years ago.

Apollo°° that brought you onto the earth
rests majestically beside you.

At the very moment, the round moon
was snooping out of the window,

so, I stood aside to let her
take a quick look at the rock.

° The virginial Roman goddess of the moon and the hunt.

°° The US spacecraft designed to explore the moon. Apollo 11 made the first historic moon landing in July 1969.

물 한 옹큼

맑디맑은
물 한 옹큼

하늘이 있고
구름이 있네

어디를 어떻게
얼마나 돌고 돌면
이렇게 맑아지나

한 옹큼
순수를

달디 달게
마시네.

A Handful of Water

A handful of water is
as clear as it can be.

The sky and the clouds
are adrift on it.

Where, how, and how many rounds
should it orbit around to turn
crystal-clear like this?

In a handful of
crystalline purity,

I drink
as if it's nectar.

우리 개 양순이

웃기기 잘하는 친구가 찾아와
흙마당에 자는 듯 누워 있는 양순이를 보고
자기가 와도 아는 채를 않는다고
'불학무식'하다고 험욕을 해댔다.

땅을 요 삼고 하늘을 이불 삼고
와선(臥禪)에 든 건지 적정(寂靜)에 든 건지
좌망(座忘)을 하는 건지 오상아(吾喪我)의 경지인지
달관도 같고 해탈도 같다.

"자네 눈이 삐었네.
대낮에 사람 드나드는 마당 한가운데
땅바닥에 배 붙이고 '오불관언'하는 경지
자네 저만큼 초탈할 수 있나?

양순이는 불학무식이 아니라
절학무위(絶學無爲)!
저렇게 되자면 나는 백 년,
자네는 한 오백 년은 걸리겠지."

Yangsun, **Our Dog**

Once, a funny friend called on me
and looked at *Yangsun*. It was lying down
    as if sleeping on the ground.
He abused at the dog because it played dumb;
he decried it as an utter ignoramus.

Regarding the earth as a mattress
    and the sky a duvet,
it seems to have entered into 'meditation in a supine
    position', or nirvana, or self-oblivion, or superego,
or to have obtained a farsighted view, or salvation.

You are a proper fool.
Amid the courtyard where people come and go
in a broad daylight, can you arrive at a state of
disinterestedness like the dog?

Yangsun *is not an ignoramus*
but above any learning or knowledge!
To reach a stage of Yangsun's, *I may need*
    one hundred years,
but more than five hundred years be taken for you.

선(禪)

TV 앞에 앉았는데 아내가
당신 뭐해요?
TV 봐.
켜지도 않구요?
응, 켜줘.

밥상머리에 앉으니 아내가
TV에 뭐 나왔어요?
몰라
보구도 몰라요?
글쎄, 기억이 안 나네.

아내는 내가 피곤해서라 하고
친구 놈은 내가 치매라고 악담하고
돌중은 나더러 도통한 거나 아닌가 하고
의사는 나더러 건망증 같다는데

Seon°

When I sat in front of the TV,
my wife asked, *What are you doing?*
I replied, *Watching the TV.*
Not turning it on?
Yeah, turn it on for me, please.

On sitting at the dining table,
my wife asked, *What was on the TV?*
I don't know, I replied.
Don't know, even though you watched it?
Well, I can't remember.

My wife says I'm tired;
yet, my friend derides I'm in dementia.
A wandering monk wonders I might have
    obtained enlightenment;
yet, a doctor says I'm amnestic.

° A Korean Buddhist meditation.

약간은 맞고 약간은 틀리고
어쩌면 모두 맞고 어쩌면 모두 틀리는

이것을 나는 걱정하지 않는다.
자주 난 이런 한때를 즐기고 싶다.

When part of their words is correct
    and part incorrect,
or when perhaps all of their words are
    either correct or incorrect,

I'm not worried about this.
Often, I wish to relish this sort of occasions.

이 또한 지나가리라

흘러가거라
우리 여기 강 언덕에서
근심스레 보고 있나니
세차고 어지러운 탁류여
어서 흘러가다오.

바윗돌 굴리며
내리미는 물머리가 오면
크고 작은 물고기들 물가로 밀려 나와
강물 맑아지도록 기다리듯이

기다리자, 바닷새처럼
바위섬 벼랑 끝에 둥지 튼 괭이갈매기처럼
성난 바다, 질풍노도 내려다보며
날 개고 바다 자도록 기다리듯이

세상이 칸막이 없는 동물원 되어
서로 물고 뜯고 쌈질만 할 때는,
미친 좀비 떼가 몰려다닐 때는
피하는 수밖에 도리가 없구나.

This Too Shall Pass Away

Flow away.
Overlooking a river on the hill,
we keep a watchful eye
on the violent, chaotic and murky water.
Quickly, run away.

If the thrusting head of the running water
    jostles along while rolling rocks,
the big or small fish driven out
to the edge of the river
are waiting until the water gets clean,

let us wait like a seabird, a black-tailed sea gull
nested on the edge of a cliff in a rocky island,
looking down an angry sea or a storm or a gale
until the weather clears up and the sea gets calm.

When the world turns into a zoo without partition,
when animals are only biting and ripping, and
when a crowd of crazy zombies go round in groups,
there is no other choice but to flee.

아득한 옛날부터
더럽고 기막힌 세상 있어 왔고
그래도 우리 용하게 살아남았거니
지금이나 앞으로도 그러할 거니

새삼스런 일 아니라오
지진도 해일도 끝이 있나니
'이 또한 모두 지나가리라.'
우리 여기 담담히 기다리다 가리라.

지나가라.
시궁창아,
어서 썩 멀리 흘러가거라.

From the remote past,
there has been a murky, dumbstruck world;
yet we have managed to stay alive splendidly
and are to keep going in the future as ever.

There is nothing new;
an earthquake or a tsunami has also an end.
These too shall pass away.
Calmly, we will wait here and go off.

Pass away,
a cesspit—
quickly, run far away.

봄소식

버들개지 사진 찍어
카톡으로 보냈더니

서울선 시위대 사진이
시리즈로 왔네.

봄이 와도 봄이 온 줄
모를 것 같아

매화가지 여러 장 찍어
다시 보낸다.

Tidings of Spring

After I sent the picture
of a pussy willow by KaTalk,

a series of protesters' pictures
came back from Seoul.

As they seem unaware
of the advent of spring,

I send a few pictures of
plum sprigs over KaTalk again.

카톡이나

우리 절대 만나질랑 말아요.
아주 센 자석처럼 바로 붙겠죠.
그러고는 감당 못해 후회하겠죠.
그러니 카톡이나 주고받아요.
젊을 적 사진 있음 보여 주구요.
그러다가 오랫동안 소식 없으면
이젠 핸폰도 못쓰나 생각하겠죠.
언젠간 알겠죠, 어쩜 모를 꺼예요.
나는 당신이, 당신은 내가
오래 전 이 세상에 없었다는 것을.

Let's Rather Talk over KaTalk

Let's never meet with each other
or we'll stick at once like a strong magnet.
Then, we'll regret for being not up to it.
So, let's rather talk over KaTalk.
If you have a photo in your youth,
    send it to me.
Meanwhile, if there is no news from me for years,
you may suppose now I'm unfit for a cellphone.
Someday, you may or may not know;
a long time before, I was not in this world
as you might not be here as well.

고사관수도(高士觀水圖)

모자 따윈 필요 없다.
오늘 하루는 백수(白首)가 되자.

세상은 깎아지른 석벽같이
날이 서고 삼엄하지만

옷고름도 풀고
너럭바위에 엎으러져

고인 듯 흐르는 물을
내려다 보자.

명경 같은 수면에 청산도 멋 있고
청산이 바람결에 흔들리는 것도 좋지만

이 평화와 고요 속에
말없이 있고 싶다.

흐르다 고인 물에 눈을 주고서
보이면 보고 안 보여도 좋고

The Picture of a Hermit Who Gazes on Water

There is no room for a hat and the like;
today, one day only, no hat.

Like a precipitous rocky wall,
the world is sharply edged and harsh, though.

Untying a coat string
and facing down with hands on flat rocks,

he gazes into the running water
seemingly unmoving.

Though on the crystalline clear water,
    the green mountain looks splendid
and its waving in the wind is another sight,

but in peace and serenity,
he wishes to remain without a word.

Setting his eyes on the stagnant water,
if visible, he'd look; if not, he'd not care.

그냥 그저 그러다가 해 저물 때까지
물과 어둠이 하나 될 때까지
보이면 보고 안 보여도 좋고.

Idling away his day until dusk
or until water and darkness are united—
if visible, he'd look; if not, he may not care.

이 가을, 문득

이 가을
하늘은 높다 못해 푸르르고
곱디고운 단풍 속을 나는 걷는다.
아, 여기가 바로 낙원이구나!

저 무한 우주의 무수한 별들 중에
오직 하나 푸른 보석, 지구별에
내가 생겨나 살아가고 있다는 게
신기하고 다행하고 고맙기 그지없다.

비록 인생이
더러는 힘들고
때로는 억울하고
아무리 아까워도

이 아름다운 별에 태어나
이 따스한 별에 살다가
이 포근한 별에 묻히는 것만으로도
생명은 얼마나 복된 것인가!

머나먼 안드로메다에도 숨 쉴 곳 없다는데

Unexpectedly, This Autumn

This autumn,
the sky is so high that it can't be but azure blue.
I take a stroll amid the splendid autumn foliage.
Ah, this is a paradise!

Among the myriad planets in a boundless space,
I'm wondrous, lucky, grateful beyond words
for dwelling on this singular blue gem-like earth
from which my life came into being.

Life is
sometimes harsh,
often resentful,
and as much as pitiful, though;

if one, born in this lovely planet,
had lived on this warm star,
and were just buried on this snug earth,
what a blessing his life would be!

They say there is no place to breathe

물이 있고 꽃이 피고 새가 나는
여기 밖에 따로 천국이 없다는 걸
이 가을 문득 깨닫고 보면

땅 위에 뭇 생명 가진 것들과
더불어 사랑하고 즐겁게 살리라.
그리고 죽음이란 것도 한없이 정겨운
낙원의 품으로 돌아가는 것 다름 아니랴.

in far-off Andromeda.
Suddenly this autumn, I realize
there is no paradise save for here—
where water runs, flowers blow, and birds fly.

Along with all living things on earth,
I wish to live in love and glee.
Then, death is nothing but going back
to the bosom of an infinitely intimate paradise.

안동역

잠이 안 와
밤거리에 나서면
내 발자국 소리 들으며
가는 곳이 있어 좋았다.

찻집도 술집도
불이 꺼지고
도시에 가장 큰 쇼핑몰도
문이 닫기면

가는 곳은 기차역
TV가 있는 대합실.

오는 손님 가는 손님
기다리는 손님
말을 나눌 손님이 있어 좋았다.

텅빈 대합실
TV 앞에서 졸기도 하던

낼 모래 그 역마저

Andong Train Station

At a sleepless night,
if I go out to the night streets,
it is nice that I could go there,
listening to my own footfall.

When light was turned off
at tea shops or pubs
and when the largest mall
was closed,

there was a waiting room with TV
at the station where I used to pop in.

It was nice because there were comers,
goers, and awaiters with whom
I could strike up a conversation.

It was also the vacant waiting room
where I used to doze in front of TV.

Tomorrow or the day after tomorrow,

멀고 외진 송현동으로 옮긴다 한다.
이젠 너무 멀어 갈 수가 없다.

고요한 밤거리
내 발자국 소리 들으며 찾아가는
기차역이 있어 좋았다.

the station has been said to move
    to far remote Songhyeon-dong°.
Now, I can't go there; it's too far to walk.

In the quiet streets at night,
it was nice that I could go to the station,
listening to my own footfalls.

° The Andong station located at the center of the city moved to the new station at Songhyeon-dong on the 17th of December in 2020. The old station has had a history of ninety years.

마스크를 쓰고

오늘도 마스크를 쓰고
바람 부는 강둑길을 걷는다.
마주 오던 젊은이가
마스크를 쓴 채 눈인사를 한다.
반가운 얼굴
허나 우린 멈칫멈칫 악수도 않고
비끼어 간다.
언제까지 우린 이래야 하나
지척에 갇힌 사랑하는 사람아
죽음을 무릅쓰고 만나고 싶지만
조심하자고
조금만 더 견뎌 보자고
강둑에 서서 간절한 문자를 보낸다.

Putting on a Mask

Today, too, putting on a mask,
I walk along the windy riverbank.
In opposite, a young man with a mask
nears and greets me with eyes.
A familiar face.
Yet we pass by hesitantly
without shaking hands.
How long do we have to do this way?
At the risk of my life, I want to see
my love locked up within a foot, though;
Let's stay on alert,
let's put up with a bit longer.
On the bank, I send an ardent text message.

5부
Part Five

Uncollected Poems

편지

—원이 아빠에게

당신이 내게
검은 머리 파뿌리 되도록
함께 살다 죽자 하시더니
어찌하여 나를 두고 당신 먼저 가시나요
나랑 아이들 다 버리고
당신 혼자 가시나요.

함께 누워 당신께
남들도 우리같이 서로
어여뻐하고 사랑할까 물었더랬죠.
어찌 그 일 잊으시고 먼저 가시는가요.
당신 없이는 살 수 없으니
날 데려가 주세요.

뱃 속 아기는 누구더러
아버지라 부르라는 건가요.
당신은 거기 가면 그만이지만
아무리한들 내 마음 같을까요
한도 끝도 없는 내 설움
다 못 쓰고 대강만 적습니다.

*원이 엄마의 편지를 리메이크하다.

A Letter[○]

—To Wonni's Daddy

You said to me, *Let's get along*
until our black hair turns to
the white root of a green onion;
yet, how come you go ahead—
beleaving both me and little halves
and going off by yourself!

Whilst lying down with you,
I asked whether others too adore
and love each other like us.
How could you forget that and go first?
Without you, I cannot live on;
please take me along with you.

To an unborn baby in my belly,
whom is he told to call a daddy?
Once you get there, that's it, though;
no matter how sad you are,

○ In 1998, a grave was excavated from the construction site for the new residential area in Andong city. The occupant of the grave was identified as Yi Eung-tae (1556-1586) who died at the age of 30. His bereft wife left a letter to her husband in the coffin. But she was not identified, except that the young woman is the mother of Wonni and an unborn child. The letter is a literal transcription in the modern vernacular.

이 편지 자세히 보시고
꿈에 와서 당신 모습 보여 주세요.
나는 꿈에 당신을 볼 수 있어요.
몰래 와서 만나 주세요.
하고 싶은 말 끝이 없으나
눈물이 앞을 가려 더 쓸 수가 없네요.

would it be the same as my heart?
Not spelling out my grief with neither
bounds nor end, I jot it down tersely.

After perusing this letter,
come in my dream and let me view you.
I can see you in my dream;
sneak in my dream and meet me.
There's no end to what I want to say—
since tears flood from my eyes,
I can't go on writing.

얄리얄리 얄라셩 얄라리 얄라

고려 때 슬픈 노래
청산별곡 끝에
<얄리얄리 얄라셩 얄라리얄라>
이게 무슨 뜻인지 나는 몰라도

반야심경 맨 끝에 후렴같은 반복
<아제아제 바라아제 바라승아제>
희한하게 리듬이 닮았단 생각.

노래의 후렴이 다라니를 닮다니,
왜 닮았는지는 나는 몰라도
그냥 그저 그렇다는 생각이 든다.

얄리얄리 얄라셩 얄라리얄라
아제아제 바라아제 바라승아제

고려 때라 노래도
염불 닮았남?

Yal-li-yal-li yal-la-sheong yal-la-ri yal-la

At the end of *Cheongsan-byeolgok*[°],
a mornful song of the Gyoreo dynasty,
comes *Yal-li-yal-li yal-la-sheong yal-la-ri yal-la.*
I have no idea what it means, though,

a repeat like a refrain at the end of Heart Sutra—
Aje-aje bara-aje bara-seung-aje[°°]—occurs to me
that its rhythm is strangely similar to the end of
    Cheongsan-byeolgok.

How the song's refrain can echo a dharani!
I do not know how it can happen that way.
I just reflect that it is just so-so.

Yal-li-yal-li yal-la-sheong yal-la-ri yal-la:
Aje-aje bara-aje bara-seung-aje.

Since it was sung during the Goryeo dynasty,
did it resemble the prayer to Buddha?

[°] *Cheongsan-byeolgok* is one of the vernacular poems of the late Goryeo dynasty. The vernacular poems are known as Goryeo gayo. It is a general term for various lyrics, including folk songs, court dance music adapted from folk songs, Buddhist songs, and shaman chants. Buddhism was a national religion during the Goryeo dynasty.

[°°] The end of Heart Sutra reads in Chinese as "揭諦揭諦波羅揭諦波羅僧揭諦". The line is the transcription of Korean pronunciation of the Chinese characters. In translation, it may be rendered: "Gone, gone, gone to the other shore beyond."

2월아, 고맙다.

빨리
버들개지 피는 봄을 맞으라고
29, 30, 31일을
뭉청 잘라 주는구나.

2월아,
고맙다.

(2021. 2. 28)

Thanks, February

To meet quickly
    with spring that brings
a blossoming pussy willow,
the 29th, 30th, and 31st day in February
are cut off in a lump!

Thanks,
February.

(28 February 2021)

산처(山妻)

뉴스를 보고 나더니
아내가

우리가 걱정할 건
하나도 없네요, 한다.

그러게 내 뭐랬나,
아무 걱정 말라니까,

그게 다 내 덕인 줄
이제 조금 아나 몰라.

(2021. 3)

A Woodsman's Wife

Watching the news on TV,
my wife said:

There's nothing for us
to worry about.

Yeah, what I did say:
Don't worry at all.

I wonder whether she has known
a little that's all thanks to me.

(March 2021)

골분(骨粉)

갑자기 핸드폰에 부고가 떴다.
정말일까,
떨리는 손으로 버튼을 눌러본다.

그의 아내가 훌쩍이며
오지 말라고 한다.

나도 목 멘 소리로
핸드폰이라도 함께 묻어주라 했다.
내 정신이 아니었다.

멀쩡하던 사람이 연기가 되어
굴뚝을 빠져 하늘로 가다니!

말 못하는 재만
한 됫박 남겨 놓고.

(2021. 4)

Bone-dust

Suddenly, an obituary notice popped up
    on my cellphone.
Is it true?
I pressed the botton with trembling hands.

His sobbing wife replied:
Do not come, please.

In a chocked voice,
I uttered: *Bury even a cellphone with him.*
I was out of my mind.

What in the world a friend who was well
turned to white smoke and went up
    to heaven through a stack!—

leaving behind a gourd bowl
of speechless dust only.

(April 2021)

버들치

계곡에 옹달샘은 차고 말갛다.
버들치야. 쬐그만 버들치야.
넌 어쩌려고 이 외진 곳에
몰래 살고 있느냐.

배고플 텐데,
외로울 텐데.

(2021. 10)

A Minnow

In a dell, springwater is cold and clear.
A minnow, a wee minnow.
How come you are living covertly
in the middle of nowhere.

You may be hungry
and lonely, I am afraid.

(October 2021)

다시 작별을 위해

—아리아를 위하여

살아 있어야 해요.
그대 깊은 눈 들여다 보고
옛날처럼 뜨거운 입술 닿게 해줘요.

살아 주어야 해요.
세월이 빨리 흘러
세상에 아무도 우리 둘 아는 이 없을 때

새로 만나, 옛말하며
흰 머리칼 쓰다듬게 해줘요.
그대 물 어린 눈 들여다 보게 해줘요.

아, 그렇게라도 하지 않고
그대는 거기서, 나는 여기서
어떻게 모르는 사람처럼 따로 갈 수 있나요.

사랑한다고
남은 날까지 사랑할 거라고
예전에 못다 한 말 속삭이게 해줘요.

그리고 나도 떠나게 해줘요.

(2021.6)

To Bid a Farewell Again

—For an aria

You should stay alive.
Let me look in your deep eyes as in old days
and let my burning lips touch yours.

You should keep on living.
Days go so fast;
when no one knows you and me,

let us meet again and talk over old days.
Let me pat your hair
and look in your dewy eyes.

Alas, without doing so in such a way—
from where you are or where I am,
how we can depart separately like strangers.

Let me love you
until the end of my life. Let me whisper
in words unspoken in old days

and then, let me go.

(June 2021)

6부
Part Six:

Autobiographical Essay:
My Life and My Literature

I

On 27 November 1942, I was born at my mother's parents' home in a village called Uiyang-ri, Chunyang-myeon, Bongwha-gun, Gyeongsangbuk-do, Korea, as the eldest son of seven children of Kim Gu-jik (金九稷, 1921-2014) and Kwon Yeong-im (權寧姙, 1918-1984). Born to the family clan of Uiseong Kim, I was the 13th descent of Kim Bang-geol (金邦杰, 1623-1695), whose art name was Jichon (芝村), a Confucian scholar and high ranking government official from King Hyeonjong (1641-1674) to King Sukjong (1661-1720) during the Joseon dynasty. After passing the civil service exams in 1660 and taking a variety of governmental or local positions, he served King Sukjong (1661-1720), the 19th king of the Joseon dynasty, as head of National Confucian Academy, higher educational institute, and head of saganwon (Office of the Censor-General). After the end of the Korean War in 1953, my father who graduated from the College of Law, Sungkyunkwan University, took a job in Daegu as a police officer. At eleven, I had to leave my father's old house inherited from ancestors and located at a village called Jirye, Imdong-myeon, Andong city. Along with my family, I moved to Daegu, the largest city in Gyeongsangbuk-do.

II

When I was a student in middle school in the early 1950s, apart from compulsory subjects, students were required to choose an extracurricular subject for an independent study. I decided to study literature and joined a literary club. If I acted on the advice of my father who was always anxious about my health, I should have to join either a taekwondo team or a gymnastic club. However, it seemed to me that the literary club would provide me with a good chance to learn something about literature, and a literary study appeared congenial to my disposition. In my childhood, I spent much time with my grandfather in his guest room and was impressed by his literary conversation with his guests. At that time, I reckoned vaguely that literature must be a highly valuable subject of study to pursue. Perhaps, this early experience might have helped me to choose literature as an extracurricular study in my middle school days.

Retrospectively, what I listened in on my grandfather's conversation with his visitors was about my ancestor, Kim Bang-geol as well as other prominent literary figures from ancient China as well as the Joseon dynasty. My grandfather who was educated in Confucianism was well versed in Chinese and Korean classics in his own way. Their conversation ranged over the story of "Shangri-la" (武陵桃源) by the Chinese poet and politician, Tao Yuanming (365~427), "Red Cliffs' Rhapsody" (赤壁賦) by Su Shi (蘇軾, 1037-1101), and satrical poems by Kim Byung-yeon (1807-1863) who was better known as Kim Sat-gat in the late Joseon dynasty. In one of the poems composed by Kim Bang-goel, there is my favorite line; "I behold the blue mountains all day long with no one to talk to" (終日無言對碧岺)[1]. My grandfather often went out of the house. When he was not at home, I was left alone to look after the house. What I did often at that time was to look at the mountains in front of our house, whilst propping my chin on the threshold and murmuring my ancestor's as well as Kim Byeong-yeon's poems. What minstrel Kim Sat-gat's poem enthralled me was his witty and satirical bent as in his well-known poem, "A Bowl of Gruel".

In a bowl of gruel on a four-legged pine tray,
A shadow of clouds in the sky is adrift.
Host, don't be sorry for watery gruel.
I love a blue mountain mirrored on water.

四脚松盤粥一器
天光雲影共排徊
主人莫道無顔色
吾愛青山倒水來[2]

네 다리 소반 위에 멀건 죽 한 그릇.
하늘에 뜬 구름 그 속에서 함께 떠도네.
주인이여, 면목이 없다고 말하지 마오.
물속에 비치는 청산을 내 좋아한다오.

This witty, satirical poem has been a great comfort for my life journey. Indeed, some of my poems were indirectly written

1) His poem is quoted from a poem titled "mueonje" (無言齊) in Kim Bang-geol's *Collected Writings* vol. 1. This volume was originally published in 1895.

under the influence of the renowned minstrel, Kim Sat-gat, whose family origniated from Andong in my home city. But he did not belong to our family clan.

From my grandfather's conversation, I also overheard about "Red Cliffs' Rhapsody" by Su Shi. He is better known by his art name Dongpo (東坡). In Korea, he has been widely regarded as one of the most accomplished figures in classical Chinese literature. He was not only a poet but also a statesman during the Northern Song dynasty in China. It is well known that Dongpo composed his famous "Red Cliffs' Rhapsody" in 1082, while travelling on a small boat to visit the Red Cliffs in an autumn night during his first exile in Hungzhou. Like him, my ancestor Jichon also composed his own poem in his later life by the river "Red Cliffs" during his exile at Dongbok, Hwasun-gun, Jellado. From time to time, my grandfather was used to recite the poem for his visiting guests:

> This autumn in the year of *gapsul* appears
> the same as the autumn in the year of *imsul*.
> A banished vassal comes here to make merry
> where the banished vassal made merry.
> The tints of a thing that existed in a thousand
> years ago are aslo omnipresent here—
> The boat is full of the bright moonlight

2) Heo Gyeong-jin, *Chinese Poems in Korea: Selected Poems of Kim Lip* (『한국의 한시: 김립시선』), trans. Seoul: Pyeongminsa, 2020, 27. Kim Byeong-yeon was born in Yangju, Gyeonggi-do in 1807 and died in 1863. After discovering the tragic death of his grandfather who surrendered to the rebel Hong Gyeong-rae during the reign of King Sunjo, he lost hope in the mundane world. With a hat on head and a bamboo cane in hand, he wandered all over Joseon for more than 30 years. Posthumously, his first collected volume was published in 1939, but the 1941 enlarged edition includes 343 poems.

and the fresh wind.

甲戌秋同壬戌秋
逐臣遊處逐臣遊
千年物色分留在
明月淸風滿小舟[3)]

갑술년(甲戌年) 이 가을이 임술년(壬戌年)만 같구나
쫓겨난 신하 놀던 곳에 쫓겨난 신하가 와서 노네.
천년 전 물색이 여기에도 있는데
밝은 달 맑은 바람이 배에 가득하구나.

In the autumn of the *gapsul* year (1694), the banished high-ranking government official Kim Bang-geol went boating in the river "Red Cliffs" in Hwasun. His experience of boating in exile must have reminded him of another banished poet, Su Dongpo, who was in a situation similar to him by boating at Red Cliffs in exile in the autumn of the *imsul* year (1082). These two episodes are juxtaposed and congmegrated in this poem. From my early childhood, I was acquainted with these episodes through my grandfather and immersed in such a literary dialogical milieu into which my grandfather unwittingly ushered me. When I grew up, I came to believe that my familial literary background helped me fashion my own literary style. Unconsciously, I believe that this familial background has led me to love poetry and to choose a literary club for my extracurricular activity. Nonetheless, through the extracurricular study, I had never completed a piece of work during the middle-school years. Other fellow students seemed

3) Quoted from Kim Bang-geol's *Collected Writings*, Vol. 1.

to write easily their own creative pieces, and subsequently to have won literary prizes as well. But that was not my case. To me, their works seemed neither laudable nor satisfactory at all. Simply, they were far below my own literary criteria. I could hardly praise their works because my eyes were set on such famous works appeared in the Korean language textbook as "Cheongnoru" (A Green Roe Deer) by Mok-wol Park[4)], "Beside a Chrysanthemum" by Jeong-ju Seo[5)], and "Monk's Dance" by Ji-hun Jo[6)]. For me, writing a good piece of my own work was just wishful thinking at the time. I had no proper guiding teacher nor creative writing education. Anyhow, that was the end of my earliest futile attempt to write a creative work in my middle school years.

III

In the meantime, my father who was deeply concerned

---

4) Park Mok-wol was born in Goseong-gun in 1916, but raised in Gyongju. He made literary debut as poet in 1939 and is best known as one of the poets of *Cheongnokpa* along with Jo Ji-hoon (1920-1968) and Park Du-jin(1916-1998). He died in Seoul in 1978..

---

5) Seo Jeong-ju was born in Gochang, Jellabuk-do in 1915. He began his career as a poet in the middle of the 1930s. He made his literary debut as a poet in 1936. Two years later, he created a sensation in the poetry world by bringing out *Whasajip* (花蛇集). After liberation from Japanse rule in 1945, he taught Korean literature at several universities and retired in 1979. He was a professor emeritus of Dongguk University. He was the most important poet and was the most profound and versatile poetic voice in his day. As poetry editor of *Hyundae Munhak,* he brought out a large number of promising young poets. He died in 2001.

---

6) Jo Ji-hun was born in Yeongyang-gun, Gyeongsangbuk-do, in 1920. He made a literary debut in 1940. He taught at Korea University and died in 1968. He is known as one of the poets of *Cheongnokpa* (靑鹿派).

about my health urged me to go to a gymnasium to improve my health. Through a hard training at the gymnasium, I became a gymnastic athlete. But I did not neglect to read literary works which I borrowed from the public library. Consequently, my academic records in the middle-school years turned to be poor. So, I could not go to a public high school. Instead, I was recruited as a talented gymnastic student for a private gymnastic high school. In my first year of high school, I was approached by my Korean language teacher who kindly urged me to enter a school poetry competition. At the contest, unexpectedly I won the first prize by writing a poem called "Yeolmae" (Fruit). This poem echoes Seo Jeong-ju's poem titled "Hwasa (花蛇)" (Asian Tiger Snake) from *Selected Poems of Jeong-ju Seo.* Many years later after revisions, I changed the original title "Yeolmae" of the poem to "Gwawonugam" (果園有感), and put it into my first volume of collected poems published in 1974. Here goes my revised poem of "Gwawonugam":

> *". . . if a man looks at a woman lustfully, he has*
> *already committed adultery with her in his heart."*
> Due to an uneasy precocity of nineteen,
> Repeating words from Matthew's fifth chapter
> And entering an orchard in the placid autumn
> sunshine,
> I have the choking sensuality of bursting fruit.
> At last, I decode the coquetry of Venus;
>
> All at once,
> Caught by a sudden desire for biting,

I stick deeply my teeth into the fruit,
Heavens!
A sin of Eve and a remorse of Eve . . . .

If I stir up delusion
And swallow a piece of the fruit—
Hee he he he he he he he he he he he hee;
Laughter of a snake passing after grinding brain.
Meanwhile,
Did you ever get ready for another sin?[7)]

It was at the age of sixteen when I wrote "Yeolmae" for the school poetry contest. I thought that it must have bewildered the judging panelists. At that time in Daegu, there was a lending public library called "Namsan Library" close to my house. From the library, I loaned many books and read such books as *Cheongma Sijib* by Yu Chi-whan[8)], *Barley Pipe* by Han Ha-un[9)], *Collected Poems of Seo Jeong-ju,* Goethe's *The Sorrows of Young Werther* (1774), Turgenev's *First Love* (1860), Dostoevski's *Poor Folk* (1945), Emily Brontë's *Wuthering Heights* (1847), André Gide's *Strait is the Gate* (1909), Hermann Hesse's *Demian: The Story of Emil Sinclair's Youth* (1919), and Anne Frank's *The Diary of Anne Frank* (1959). These books were not easily

7) The title of this poem was again changed to "Kwawoneseo (In the Orchard)" when the poem was collected in *Jeokmakhaeng* (寂寞行) in 1999.

8) Yu Chi-hwan was born in Geoje-gun, Gyeongsangnam-do in 1908. He studied at Yonhui Libral Arts College, but left without a degree. He made debut as a poet in 1931. He died of a car accident in Pusan in 1967.

9) Han Ha-un was born in Hamheung-gun, Hamgyeongnam-do, in 1920. He moved from North to South in 1948. He suffered from leprosy throughout his life. He died in 1975.

accessible to a general reader at that time. Of course, these books had enormously enhanced not only my perception of humanity but also helped me to set my goal in my life. Vaguely, my ambition was to write such a masterpiece which is well known in the world literature. Soon, I had made my mind to write a great work as soon as possible, even though I did not know how.

As a gymnastic student at high school, however, my life did not allow me to indulge in what I wanted to do. My school life was divided into two parts. In the morning, I had a regular classroom work. In the afternoon, however, routinely I had to go to the gymnasium to prepare for competition. Completely fed up with school life, I just dropped out of the gymnastic high school after two-year and half. In September 1958, my family had to move back from Daegu to my hometown, Andong city when my father resigned his job in Daegu. He told me to decide whether I would stay in Daegu or come along with him. I decided to go to Andong with my family. At last, I could escape from the horribly hard training for a gymnast. I was transferred to a new public school in Andong with which I was unfamiliar.

After arrival in Andong, I found that because my family were large, I could not have my own room to study at home. So, I had to move to a boarding house near my school. At the boarding house, I started to write a novel. A novel about a tragic love was my secret ambition. My best friend's sister was adopted as a heroine in my novel. Just like *Wuthering Heights* by Emily Brontë, who never had a love affair, I attempted to write about a romantic and tragic love. In fact, writing a novel was a reckless attempt for a complete novice.

In the meantime, my family assumed that I was devoting myself to the preparation of university admission examinations. On the contrary, I didn't pay any attention to university admission. For me, the most urgent and supreme task was to write a novel which would shake the world, not to go to a university. I consoled myself with an idea that there have been many writers who wrote masterpieces before they reached the age of twenty. For example, Anne Frank[10] (1929-1945) was fourteen years old when she started to write her diary in 1942 and ended her last entry for the diary on 1 August 1944. Raymond Radiguet[11] (1903-1923) was seventeen when he published the novel *Le Diable au Corps* in 1923. Françoise Sagan [12] (1935-2004) was nineteen when she published her first novel *Bonjour Tristesse* in 1954.

"If I begin to write a novel now," I imagined, "I might be just over twenty by the time I finish it up". Feeling desperate, I worked hard all night long like a normal high school student preparing for the university entrance exams. From time to time, I was absent from school for my writing. However hard I worked, there was no visibly significant improvement worthy to mention. Without practice nor a proper education for a creative writing, I felt so much lack of confidence about what I wrote. The books I had read were almost all translated works

10) She was a German-Dutch diarist of Jewish heritage. She was one of the most discussed Jewish victims of the Holocaust during the Second World War. Posthumously, she became famous for her *Diary of a Young Girl* in 1947. She died at the age of 15.

11) He was a French novelist and poet who became famous for his two novels; *Le Diabe au corps* (The Devil in the Flesh) in 1923 and *Le bal du Comte d'Orgel* (The Ball of Count Orgel) in 1924.

12) She was a French playwright, novelist and screenwriter. She is best known for her first novel, *Bongjour Tristesse*, published in 1954 when she was a teenager.

published originally in the Western world. Thus, whatever I wrote about turned to be a style of translated works. In my writing, I was strictly adhering to Gustave Flaubert's dictum of prose style, the principle of finding "le mot juste" (the right word), as my own golden rule. This principle made me revise unceasingly what I had written until I was completely satisfied.

In the meantime, my graduation day from high school was coming near, but I was utterly unprepared for the examinations of university admission. Above all, my novel was undone and ended up finally with a total disaster. I had a nervous breakdown and fell into an abnormal state of mind.

On a bitter cold day in winter, my parents found me almost fainted away in an unheated room at the boarding house. They wrapped my books and belongings up, and moved them to my parents' home in the city. When the winter vacation came, they sent me to the house of my relative in Daegu. Living there, I had to study at a private institute for university entrance examinations. Thus, my juvenile dream to become a novelist was completely evaporated for a while.

IV

In 1960, I was accepted to Sungkyunkwan University in Seoul where I wanted to specialize in English Language and Literature. In my spare time, again I tried to write a love story in the university library. But it was not easy to write as I hoped. At the age of nineteen or twenty in the unfamilar city, Seoul, I had to go through the national crises of the 4.19 student uprising and the 5.16 military coup. My university life was in turmoil, just as other contemporaries in universities across the nation had suffered from the same emotional and intellectual chaos. I gave up writing completely, thinking that I would find more adequate time later for a long novel.

When I was a junior in the university, I began to write a short poem. But it was not easy for me to write even a short piece. Hoping to produce a masterpiece, I revised a work again and again after I finished it. Sometimes, I incubated a future work in my mind for several months. Meanwhile, there was a sign on campus that a poetry club called "Jiha" (Underground) was about to emerge. My fellow students, Kang U-sik, Kim Jun-sik, and Yeun Tae-su, invited me to join the club. After thorough-going revisions, I published some poems such as "An Apparition," "What does it make sense?" and "A City" which were written in this period. Later, these poems were collected in my first volume of poems in 1973.

After graduating from the university in 1965, first I worked for the *Andongsibo,* the bulletin of Andong municipal office, as an editorial staff. At that time, except for Andong Educational College in the city, culturally the city seemed blank. There was not a single cultural institute to mention. The city was a completely barren wasteland. Not a single person from the city had made a literary debut to be mentionable, as far as I knew. I myself did not make a literary debut yet. After leaving the editorial staff office, I took up a teaching job at a secondary school. While teaching at school, I recruited aspiring literary youngmen for an organized literary movement and set up Andong "munhakhoe" (The Andong Literary Society) for the first time. I was eager and ambitious to make my hometown, Andong, a cultural centre. As a result of setting up the Andong literary society, I published three issues of its coterie magazine called *Ajikdo* (Yet). In addition, perhaps the most remarkable achievement that the literary society had made was to host a poetry contest and a congratulatory performance on the occasion of unvailing a monument for the poetry of Yi Yuk-sa[13)] on the fourth of May in 1968.

My three-year teaching as well as the coterie magazine did not help me much to work upon my own writing. As usual, there was too much waste of time for miscellaneous trivia at school. Consequently, I came to a conclusion that I could not devote myself to my writing until I became a university professor. Subsequently, to work for the post-graduate program, I moved to Seoul again. In 1969, I registered as a graduate student at Konkuk University from where I received an MA in Korean Language and Literature in 1972.

V

When I was twenty-seven years old in winter, I did not return to the school from Seoul to teach in my hometown. The school was on a winter vacation. During the vacation, I made up my mind to concentrate on writing a poem. Some of my friends had already become famous after they made their

13) Born in Andong, Gyeongsangbuk-do on the 18th of May in 1904, he died at the age of 39 in the prison house attached to the Japanese consul general in Beijing on the 16th of January in 1944. His real name was Yi Won-nok, and his pen name was known as Yi Hwal or Yi Yuk-sa. He was a ferocious independent fighter against Japanese colonial rule in Korea. Although he wrote short stories and essays, he was a major figure in the literary history of the early twentieth century in Korea.

literary debut. I thought I could not wait any longer. Once I made up my mind to become a poet, I hoped to bring out a remarkable work for readers. At that time, I thought that the most distinguished poet in Korea was Seo Jeong-ju who was a professor of Dongguk University and poetry editor of *Hyundae Munhak*. My hidden covetous aspiration was to surpass his poetry. "If my poetry does not stand above his poetry", I thought, "What's the meaning of my debut?"

That year on Christmas eve, there was a heavy snowfall in Seoul. After having brunch, I put on an overcoat with its collar turned up. Then I went out to take a walk. The street was quiet in the morning. I was gradually ascending from Samseongyo[14)] towards Changkyungwon Palace, treading on the soft snow thawing slowly in the sunny side of the street. Strangely, the street seemed almost deserted. I felt refreshed and was sunk into a meditative mood, while walking along the street. My mind was jammed with numerous love stories that I had read up to the age of twenty-seven. I could not think of anything else for my work except for the theme of love. There were a countless number of love poems and love songs in the world. Yet, my emotions of loneliness and yearning were not the same as others. My illusions about love were also different from others. Thus, I thought, a love poem that I wrote should be different from that of George Gordon Byron (1788-1824) who moaned with "By that lip I long to taste;... Ζωή μου, σᾶς ἀγαπῶ (My life, I love you)"[15)], or Werther's or Napoléon's

14) This is the name of a bridge constructed over the Seongbuk brook. It was located at Dongsomun-ro bordering Seongbuk-dong. The street over the Samseongyo bridge leads to Changkyungwon Palace which was built in 1483 in the reign of King Seongjong during the Joseon dynasty.

15) Quoted from "Maid of Athens, Ere We Part" by George Gordon Byron. The Greek words, Ζωή μου, σᾶς ἀγαπῶ, are a phrase of parting which the speaker of the poem uses as a refrain.

passionate letters to his wife Josephine; "I have not spent a day without loving you; I have not spent a night without clasping you in my arms"[16). It was not easy to pinpoint what I endeavored to meditate on for my work. But I assumed that the poem must conjure up some kind of quintessential Korean emotions from a dramatic, fatal love. Thinking over these things, I was walking cautiously whilst looking down at the tips of my shoes.

All at once, I had a queer sense of something in my overcoat pocket. I put my hand in it and grasped a pack of chewing gum. When I looked back, a small old woman was looking at me with a bright smile. When I was at a loss, she said that my figure from behind looked so ponderous. My heavy gait must have been impressive to her. When I tried to return a pack of gum to her, she waved her hand dismissively and blurted, "Please, go quickly as you wish." After pushing me away, she turned her back. Her sudden interruption broke not only my pensive mood, but also irritated me. To carry on my meditation, I turned away from her. After a few steps away, realizing that I did not appreciate enough for her kindness, I turned back. But I could not find the old woman. Where did she go? Indeed, there was no one on the pavements except for my footprints on the snow. Across the street, I saw the gate of Changkyungwon Palace opened slightly. I thought that she must have gone into the Palace, but I could not find her there. On my way back home, I was searching for proper words to express my queer encounter with the street vendor through imagination. Indeed, there was nothing serious to think about, but I ventured to hypothesize the unusual encounter with the

---

16) Quoted from the letter sent by Napoléon Bonaparte to his wife, Josèphine Bonaparte, from Italy in 1796.

old woman this way:

> Perhaps in my tenth reincarnation when
> I was a cow chewing fodder at the corner of
> Kim Yu-sin's courtyard, you might have been
> a magpie alighted furtively on my back and
> flown off?

Putting the above passage as the body of a poem between an introduction and a conclusion, I began to tackle with the title of the poem. After managing to finish it up with revisions, I contributed it to "*Geulbat*" (The Field of Writings), a coterie magazine, edited by the juniors of my hometown in 1970. Then, I submitted the poem to the seventh contest for the new poems held under the auspice of the literary magazine, *Wolgan Munhak* (Monthly Literature). Some judge might have thought it queer because it was written by a young man who was less than thirty years old and the poem was uncommonly titled "To a Madam at Chwiunjeong".

In the poem, the old woman with whom I encountered in the street was transformed into a hostess at a public bar. I changed myself into a guest who visited the bar for the first time. In a former life, I imagined that I was an ox and the old woman was a magpie. Through a cycle of inscrutable reincarnation, the magpie was reincarnated into a bar hostess and the ox became a male guest to the bar. They were imagined to encounter each other in the public house.

Thus, this poem refers to as expressing either the Buddhistic idea of casual factors of cause, or an encounter between a man and a woman, or samsara, or reincarnation, or a fatal love.

Though it is a short piece, I thought it was a unique Korean love poem with a subtle nuance. Needless to say, this poem is completely different in style and tone from Western romantic love poems characterized by the passionate confession of a poet's personal emotions.

In May issue for *Wolgan Munhak* in 1970, my poem titled "To a Madam at Chwiunjeong" was announced to have been chosen for the work of a new poet as a runner-up award without a prize-winning work. Later, I was told that the late professor Kim Jong-gil[17], who was one of judges and a close relative to my family, strongly insisted that my work be chosen as a runner-up rather than a prize winning in a way to encourage. After the contest, his advice to me was "to sublate a feeling of helplessness" in my poem. For me, I was deeply unsatisfied and at the same time disappointed with his commentary. On my part, the poem is based on the idea of my own poetic techniques; the use of everyday langauge, intentionally the creation of a new rhythm as well as a supernatural world emerging from the mixture of a dream and a former life. In this way, I presumed that the poem was written according to the genuine Korean poetic tradition displayed from Hwang Jinni[18] to Seo Jeong-ju. Though I was dispirited by the runner-up award, I was determined to produce better poems. In the following year, I completed a requirement for becoming

---

17) He died on April 1, 2017. He was born in 1926 at Jirye-dong, Gilan-myeon, Andong-gun, Gyeongsangbuk-do. He was a professor of Korea University in 1958 and retired in 1992. He was a poet and translator. He published many twentieth-century British and American poetry, and also translated modern Korean poems into English.

---

18) Hwang Jin-ni (1506-1567) was a poetess, singer, and dancer in the 16th century during the Joseon dynasty. Her poetry is reputed as an exellent expression of feminine consciousness.

a poet by publishing three more poems in the March issue of *Simunhak* (Poetry). Three referees for the recommodation of my poems were Seo Jeong-ju, Sin Seok-cho[19], and Pak Du-jin[20]. Recommending words came from the mouth of Seo Jeong-ju.

Later in a private talk with the professor Seo Jeong-ju who had no chance to read "To a Madam at Chwiunjeong", I put it before him to peruse. Saying that "What a wonderfully woven text it is in terms of time and space!", he went on to express regret for losing a prize award. Then, he suggested that I should submit the poem to the monthly magazine *Hyundae Munhak* again. He added that he would contribute his own commentary on my poem to the magazine. But his comment on my poem did not appear in the magazine, solely due to my negligence of informing him about my submission to the magazine.
Seo Jeong-ju whose pen name was Midang was six years older than my father, but he always treated me on equal terms with me in courtesy, regarding me as a freak in the Korean literary circle. Afterwards, I was much indebted to his emotional support and literary guardianship for me. In fact, he was kind enough to come to Andong to officiate my wedding ceremony by making a journey from Seoul. Midang gave me my art name called Namju (南洲) and a nickname Yosan (樂山), prefaced my first collection of poems and gave a congratulatory address on

---

19) Shin Seok-cho (1909-1975) was born in Seocheon in Chungcheongnam-do. He made his literay debut as a poet in 1929. He studied philosophy in Hosei University in Tokyo, but left the university without a degree. He became the president of Korean poets' association in 1965.

---

20) Park Du-jin was born in Anseong, Gyeonggi-do in 1916 and died in 1998. He made his literary debut as a poet in 1939. He is known as one of Cheongnokpa poets.

the occasion of the publication of the first volume of poetry. Above all, he was one of screening committee members who gave me the highest mark for the qualification of professorship issued by the Ministry of Education.

VI

Throughout all my literary career, I have composed over a total of one hundred and fifty poems in number from my first year at high school up to the publication of *Melodies of Quiescence* in 2021. My output is hardly opulent; usually, I have published a couple of poems every year. This is chiefly due to my idiosyncratic habit of composing a poem. When I write a poem, I put all my energy into the work. After I finish the work, I feel always exhausted. Thus, it is not easy for me to recommence working because I need time and energy to recover from exhaustion.

Now I would like to finish my story of a literary debut which I made by contributing six poems through *Simunhak,* a vernacular poetry magazine, in 1972. These poems are "Under the Cherry blossoms", "Hometown" (故鄕), "An Apparition" (幻影), "Enlightenment" (開眼), "Chusa" (秋史), and "Requiem" (鎭魂). Among them, four poems are translated into English and included in this volume, but "Chusa" (秋史) and "Requiem" (鎭魂) are not initially included. They are first rendered into English:

Requiem (鎭魂)

If a man dies, he is buried on the mountain.
Though you are alive at that far distance,
As if letting a baby fall into sleep, who died on
mom's bosom,
You are gathered here on my bosom.

Chusa (秋史)[21)]

Someone refers to Chusa as one
who does not chime in with
what others would say.
It is not easy for me to tag along with him.

In fact, these early six poems written for my literary debut epitomize my major concerns about poetic themes throughout my whole career. The poems, "To a Madam at Chwiunjeong" and "Enlightenment", reveal my concerns about Buddhism, and "Chusa" is about Confucism. "Requiem", "An Apparition", and "Under the Cherry Blossoms" are all related in one way and another to a painful sorrow emerging out of a lost love, which has been a common subject of my poetry. From the beginning, "Hometown" was also my persistent subject which I treated in various ways.

After my literary debut as a poet, I got married in the

21) Kim Jeong-hui, whose art name is Chusa, was born in Yesan-gun, Chungcheongnam-do, in 1786. He was a reputed scholar of practical learning and a prodigious artist who produced paintings and invented a unique style of Chinese caligraphy. He died at Kwacheon, Gyeonggi-do, in 1856.

autumn of 1973. In the same year, I published my first collection of poems entitled "Enlightenment" by *Hyundaemunhaksa*. Again, Seo Jeong-ju wrote a preface to the collection and delivered a congratulatory address at the gathering to celebrate the publication of this volume. In the following year, I submitted my first collection to the judging committee for the qualification of college professorship. Without the support and recommendation of Seo Jeong-ju, I could hardly think of becoming a college professor. In March 1974, the Ministry of Education granted me the qualification of assistant professorship. After that, I began to teach at a newly established private nursing junior college in Uiseong-gun, Gyeongsangbuk-do, as an assistant professor.

Ten years later after my first volume, I published my second volume of collected poems entitled *Nae ajik jeokmake gildeulji mothae* (I'm Not Acquainted Yet with Quiescence) in 1983. This volume consists of 24 poems from the first volume and 34 new poems. The second volume containing a total of 57 poems was critically acclaimed. The late professor Pi Chyun-deuk (1910-2007) from Seoul National University encouraged me and invited me to visit him in Seoul. The poet Kim Sang-ok (1920-2004) who suffered from a stroke sent me a long encouraging letter. After he was recovered from the stroke, he came twice to see me in Andong and invited me to be a member of the revived literary magazine called *Maek* (貘). In 1992, I published the third volume entitled *Deulkkotdabal* (A Bouquet of Wild Flowers). In 2011 when I was seventy years old, I published my fourth volume of poems titled *Jirye Usa* (芝澧遺事) with 99 poems all together to commemorate my seventieth birthday. Whenever I published my new collection of poems, I revised old poems and included them in the new volume. Thus, the latest volume contains old poems which have gone through many revisions. That was an unusual habit of my composition of a poem.

Like many writers, I cannot work at all if I am not in a favorable condition for writing. To concentrate on my work, I need a proper environment. Indeed, I have tried very hard to maintain a suitable ambience. Sometimes, I have eluded either my friends to secure my own time and place to work or have moved my lodging to a new suitable place for concentration. Occasionally, even I had to change my job to make a favourable condition for my work. Meantime, to achieve my goal, I wished to be a university professor for poetry. Once I believed that becoming a professor was ideal for an aspiring young poet like me. However, my circumstances did not allow me to do my own work after I became a professor at junior college. On campus from the late 1970s to the early 1980s, I could hardly find a serene atmosphere for my work. Apart from teaching and doing research, there were so many other things to deal with in a newly estabalished private college. I thought that there were more miscellaneous works to do in the college than in the secondary schools. Apart from odd jobs, the campus was full of noises and disturbances because of students' persistent demonstrations against the corrupted college foundation at the time. College administrative professors were quite busy with non-academic affairs. Once I had taught various subjects as an instructor at a university, working for 13 hours in a week. But it was extremely difficult for me to get an appointment at a university as a full-time professor without a doctorate degree. Even though I was appointed as a professor at a university in a large city, I could not leave my hometown. After all, my domestic affairs did not allow me to take the professorship of poetry at a university in a large city.

Coda

In the later part of October in 1983, our village which had more than four hundred years of its history was under the threat of extinction by the government policy. Our village had to move to another place. Otherwise, the village could not avoid submerging by the construction of the Imha dam. At the very juncture, the famous Korean-American novelist Kim Yong-ik who was unknown to me at the time visited my village. My encounter with him changed my life completely. What he advised me was to make the best use of the ancient Korean houses just like an American Artists Colony. According to Dr Kim, the American artists' colony is detached from an urban community and very popular among the artists who need quiet environment for a creative work. For him, Jirye, my native village, was better than any American colony that he had visited. What a good advice! In fact, as the main house of the Uiseong Kim clan, it was not easy for me to decide what to do with ten ancient separate buildings and where to go. Indeed, it was even a dismaying business for me to manage them properly. If I could establish the Jirye artists' colony by moving the old houses up to the hill behind the village, it seemed to me a perfect idea to resolve a brain racking issue at that time. Because all of other residents in the village left except for my family, it would be absolutely an excellent place for artists to do their work in the quiet undisturbing environment.

Since I met Dr. Kim Yong-ik, I was quite busy building an artists' colony. With tremendous efforts, I believe I have made a remarkable achievement so far in managing an artists colony in Andong. Among various accolades, I was honoured to receive the Okgwan Order of Culture Merit from the Korean government. In the meantime, many artists and visitors across the country as well as abroad came to Jirye artists colony for their work or to relish Korean traditional culture. As part of introducing Korean culture, I have presented a foreign visitor a copy of my poems in translation. So far, my poems have been translated into four languages; English, Japanese, French and Chinese.

Up till now, I have lived in this remote woodland for over thirty years. I have become a rustic person in body and spirit. I stopped writing poems about a lost love or satirical ones. Now, my major concerns are to write about nature, eternity, and tranquility. Of nature, I wish to write poems about a serene, meditative world immune from mundane anxiety or grief in the Buddhist tradition of seon (禪) poems. I want to savour quietude by living in serenity, as I have written in "I'm Not Acquainted Yet with Quiescence", "A Crane", and "Sangmojae Pass". Perhaps, my favorite meditative mood is best expressed in "Silence".

After the moon is set
and birds are in sleep,

in silence,
I close my eyes.

Around the rims of my ears,
I hear the sound of seu-seu-seu-seu;

the sound of the quiet
rotation of

the earth
by itself.

The above poem cannot be possibly written by anyone who has no experience of living in the mountains. Of course, my poems written at Jirye for over thirty years do not deal with the same subjects and themes. Some are about love poems discarded from my school days, and others are revised poems about hope and anxiety from a wandering youth. These poems have been revised again and again before publication. I also composed narrative poems from old tales transmitted in the village from the ancient times. Along with them, I also wrote about the absurdity of human life and lamentation over a chaotic social world. In 2002, I published *Andongui Haehak* (Humour in Andong), humourous tales collected from the Andong area. In 2016, I published a collection of prose pieces under the title of *Sileul Uihayeo* (For Poetry). Finally, I am planning to write tales disappeared from Jirye village since the construction of the dam and to publish a collection of essays.

In spring 2020, realizing that I had composed a number of poems about quiescence, I collected them under the theme of quiescence. They were published under the title of *Jeeokmakhaeng* (Melodies of Quiescence). Before attaining a far-sight view, the experience of quiescence is nothing but a sense of desolation. After attaining a far-sight view, if one gets deeply acquainted with quiescence, he may transcend worldly existence and then reach a higher level of consciousness, a pure state of serenity over the mundane world. However, a poet is not a religious seeker for sainthood; his job is simply to write about the mind of a common man who aspires to reach a higher level of the transendental world.

If one lives like Tu Fu, I believe, he may write poems like Tu Fu. But I wonder who would follow Tu Fu's life to compose poems like him? I wish to write as many poems as I want, as long as I live in health and happiness. I don't believe I got used to quiescence yet. Loneliness is horrible. In my youth, I had bragged on getting through every kind of sorrow and misery in this world. Now, I know that was nothing but an act of sheer bravado. If the wind blows, it is not necessary for a bone-dry leaf to be shaken to fall. In the end, I wish to leave quietly a final volume of collected poems about quiescence.

Won-gil Kim (1942~)
Poet and Essayist

Won-gil Kim: A Chronology of His Life

1942	Born at Uiyang-ri, Chunyang-myeon, Bongwha-gun, Gyeongsang buk-do, Korea, as the eldest son of seven children.
1960-1965	Graduates from Sungkyunkwan University with a BA in English Language and Literature in Seoul.
1969-1972	Graduates from the graduate school of Konkuk University with an MA in Korean Language and Literature.
1963	Publishes the vernacular literary journal called *Jiha* (Underground) along with U-sik Kang, Jun-sik Kim, and Tae-su Yun when he was a undergraduate in Sungkyunkwan University. Contributes folk songs collected from the Andong area to the report of an academic investigation conducted by Sungkyunkwan University.
1966-1987	Teaches English and Korean at secondary schools and colleges.
1966	Founds the "Literary Society of Andong", and publishes the three issues of the society journal *Ajikdo* (Yet).
1971	Awarded the new poet prize hosted by *Wolgan Munhak* with the poem entitled "To a Madam at Chwiunjeong".
1972	Makes a literary debut as a poet recommended by Jeong-ju Seo through *Simunhak*, the sister journal of *Hyundae Munhak*.

1974	Publishes the first volume of collected poems titled *Gaean* (Enlightenment).
1975	Receives the certificate of assistant professorship for teaching at a college by passing the qualifying exams under the supervision of the Ministry of Education.
1982	Discovers a folk game called "Hahoejulbulnori" and makes public presentations at Andong Itnernational Mask Dance Festival.
1984	Publishes the second volume of collected poems titled *Nae Ajik Jeokmake Gildeulji Mothae* (I Am not Acquainted Yet with Quiescence) by Mineumsa.
1984	With the volume, awarded "Docheon Literary Prize" (1986), "Geumbok Munhwa Yesul Prize" (1988), and "Gyeongsangbuk-do Cultural Prize".
1986-2016	Founds the first Korean Artists' Colony at Jirye in Andong.
1993	Publishes the third volume of poems titled *Deulkkotdabal* (A Bunch of Wild Flowers) by Gilansa.
2002	Publishes *Andong Haehak* (Humour from Andong) by Hyonamsa.
2003	Chairs the executive committee for Andong International Mask Dance Festival.

2004	Founds the Cultural Conservatory Society for Ancient Houses and elected as the president of the society. Registers Jirye Artists' Colony in *The Michelin Guide*.
2007	Awarded the Okgwan Order of Culture Merit from the Korean Ministry of Culture and Tourism.
2009	Awarded Lee Eun-sang Literary Prize by publishing *Anaeneun Namjaro Taeeonago Sipda Handa* (Wife Wishes to Be Born As a Man) in English and Japanese translation.
2011	Publishes *Jirye Yusa*, the commemorative poetry volume for the seventieth birthday by Baum Communication.
2013	Publishes the selected poems of Won-gil Kim in French titled *Lune de Terre*, translated by Antoine Coppola.
2016	Publishes a collection of essays entitled *For Poetry*.
2016	Andong city erected a monument on which his poem is engraved in front of the Andong Arts Centre.
2016	Chairs the judging committee for Lee Sang-hwa Literary Award.
2017	Inaugurated as Dean of Andong Sinu College, an institute of Andong lifelong education. Founds Andong Literary Art College with literary courses.

2017-2019	Chairs the Gyeongbuk-do Committee of the Korea Pen Club. Awarded Gyeongbuk Pen Literary Prize.
2017	Receives the Korean Wave Grand Prize.
2020	Publishes the first edition of collected poems titled *Jeokmakhaeng* (寂寞行) by Cheongeo.
2021	Publishes the second edition of *Jeokmakhaeng* (寂寞行) by Siseonsa. This edition contains sixty-six poems taken out of eighty-six poems included in the first edition of the same title published in 2020.

About the Translator

Dr. Jeo-yong Noh studied English Language and Literature at Pusan National University for a BA (1973) and at the Graduate School of Sogang University for an MA (1977) in Seoul. He was also educated at the Graduate School of Boston College as well as Old Dominion University for his second Master's degree in English literature (1984). After his studies on American and English literature in the States, he moved to the UK in 1985 to study English literature. In 1991, he was awarded a DPhil in English literature from the University of Oxford for his study on T. S. Eliot. Since 1994, he had taught twentieth century Anglo-American poetry at Yeungnam University in Gyeongsan city, Gyeongsangbuk-do in South Korea, until his retirement in 2013.

Apart from numerous critical essays, the former professor Noh has published several scholarly books in English as well, including *Biographical Themes in T. S. Eliot's Early Poetry* (1985), *T. S. Eliot and* The Criterion (1999) and "*Action Française*" *Condemnation & Other Essays* (2003) among others. He served the T. S. Eliot Society of Korea as president from 2003 to 2005. His acclaimed English translation of Korean poems titled *Korean Buddhist Poems* was published by the Yeungnam University Press in 2006. He also translated *Omeros* by Derek Walcott (1994) and *Ronald Stuart Thomas: Collected Poems 1945-1990* into Korean for the first time (2012). Recently, he translated the *Selected Poems of Kee-Chul Lee*. The newly translated book entitled *Birds, Flowers, and Men* in parallel texts was published by the Yeungnam University Press (2019).